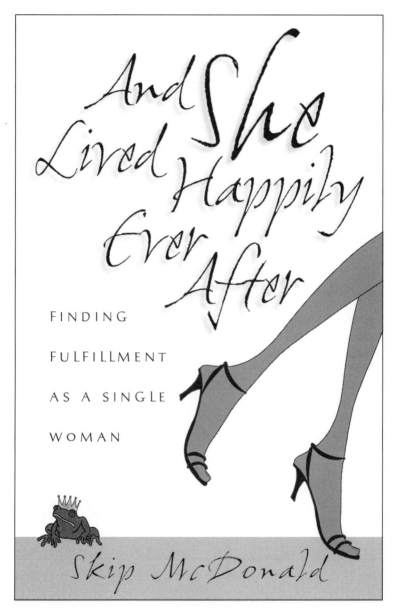

And She Lived Happily Ever After

FINDING FULFILLMENT AS A SINGLE WOMAN

Skip McDonald

InterVarsity Press
Downers Grove, Illinois

InterVarsity Press
P.O. Box 1400, Downers Grove, IL 60515-1426
World Wide Web: www.ivpress.com
E-mail: mail@ivpress.com

InterVarsity Press® is the book-publishing division of InterVarsity Christian Fellowship/USA®, a student movement active on campus at hundreds of universities, colleges and schools of nursing in the United States of America, and a member movement of the International Fellowship of Evangelical Students. For information about local and regional activities, write Public Relations Dept., InterVarsity Christian Fellowship/USA, 6400 Schroeder Rd., P.O. Box 7895, Madison, WI 53707-7895, or visit the IVCF website at <www.intervarsity.org>.

All Scripture quotations, unless otherwise indicated, are taken from the New American Standard Bible®, copyright 1960, 1962, 1963, 1968, 1971, 1972, 1973, 1975, 1977, 1995 by The Lockman Foundation. Used by permission.

Design: Cindy Kiple

Images: frog: Donna Ikkanda/Getty Images
    legs: McMillian/Getty Images

ISBN 0-8308-3265-3

Printed in the United States of America ∞

Library of Congress Cataloging-in-Publication Data

McDonald, Luberta Dian, 1955-
 And she lived happily ever after: finding fulfillment as a single
woman / Skip McDonald.
  p. cm.
 ISBN-0-8308-3265-3 (pgk.: alk. paper)
 1. Single women—Religious life. 2. Christian women—Religious
life. I. Title.
 BV4596.S5M33 2005
 248.8'432—dc22

                      2004029564

P	19	18	17	16	15	14	13	12	11	10	9	8	7	6	5	4	3	2	1
Y	19	18	17	16	15	14	13	12	11	10	09	08	07	06	05				

I dedicate this book to

Luberta Cook McDonald,

my beloved mother—who taught me

that singleness was OK.

Contents

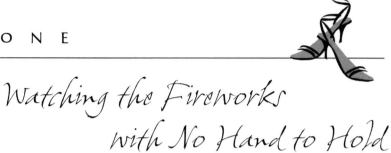

Watching the Fireworks with No Hand to Hold

I went to the Fourth of July parade with three couples. As we walked along, the couples held hands, marveling at the sights. I was keenly aware that my hand was empty.

After the parade we returned to the car. The couples were snuggling and giggling. I tried to feel included, but it wasn't working. I felt alone as I watched the sparks fly—and I'm not talking about fireworks. This was not the kind of display I had intended to watch on the Fourth!

Have you ever felt like this? Girlfriend, I know you have, or you probably wouldn't be reading this book. Welcome aboard. This is the place where we can get real with each other about the difficulties single women face.

IS SOMETHING WRONG WITH ME?

Let's face it. There are times when singleness feels like a curse. Like when loved ones tell you they "don't understand why you're not married." (How many times have you heard that one?) When you see the joy in siblings' and friends' faces as they hold their newborn babies. When you travel to see family and end up sleeping on the sofa because you're a "single" versus a "couple." When you're overlooked in making decisions because it's "just you" and you don't have a family to consider. And how about this one: when other Christians inform you that you're not married because God is teaching you submission or working something out in your life. I could go on and on. You know what I'm talking about, don't you?

It seems that single Christian women everywhere struggle with their status on some level. My friend Carol recently attended the wedding of a good friend. Although she was happy for the couple and had seen God work in their relationship, she states,

> When I saw them leave the reception talking arm in arm, I felt a mixture of joy and sadness—my good friend was happy, but she was moving five hundred miles away. The next morning grief overtook me. I silently cried out to God, "What about me?" I am part of the ranks of women with an unfilled desire for marriage. Anger at God and disappointment at being unable to find a godly man is rampant among single women in my area. Many of us bury our grief, our pain and ourselves in work and just keep hoping. We turn our desire into prayer and develop friendships. We continue living, but we want God to fulfill our desires.

Rose, a close friend for over twenty years and single by divorce, has talked to me about the pain of being misunderstood. After her marriage broke up, she says, people pointed out her sinfulness for divorcing her husband and were hurtful in other ways:

> Several relationships did not continue with my children or me, as though we had some type of disease. Some Christians seem unable to view divorce (and maybe singleness) as normal. Perhaps because God hates divorce people hate it too, and they include the person in the hatred. This has made me feel left out and almost lower class, not to mention lonely. Such comments and treatment feel like a curse.

If singleness is a curse, then more and more people are being cursed. During the last thirty years, the percentage of unmarried women ages twenty to twenty-four has doubled, according to a recent article in the *Baptist Standard*. The percentage of unmarried women in their early thirties has tripled. The pattern holds true for men as well. In 1970, 81 percent of adult men were married before their thirtieth birthday. In 2000, less than half of adult men under thirty were married. It's obvious that the single population is growing—not because of divorce, but because people are delaying marriage.

Despite the fact that singleness is becoming more and more common, the recurring theme among women seems to be that everyone should be married. And when marriage doesn't happen, many of them ask, "What's wrong with me (or her)?" Questions fly, such as:

- "Aren't you married yet?"
- "Why is a pretty woman like you still single?"
- "I'm going to pray for God to send you a husband; you need someone to take care of you."
- "Is there some hidden hurt behind why you don't want to get married?"

I have heard all of this. I have sought to answer graciously instead of slapping my interrogators. Interestingly enough, many of the people who ask me these questions are miserable in their own marriages. I don't understand it, except that maybe they would rather be miserably married than not married at all. Who will deliver us from the unhealthy need to be yoked?

Caren, one of the women of my world that I mentor, is forty-one years old. She's dealing with the reality of no longer being a young woman. Although she realizes that her dream of marriage may not happen, she remains hopeful while keeping things in perspective and living a full life. I asked her recently how she's dealing with everything. She answered, "I keep repeating Scripture. My Heavenly Father knows my need before I ask him. I try to focus on his character. I seek to stay open to whatever God has for me while getting out and doing things. I want to enjoy life by not worrying about what I don't have and being grateful for what I do have."

Are you, like Caren, honest with yourself and God about how you feel being single? Learning to lay it all before God, to get our junk out in the open where we can see it clearly, is a key part of our personal and spiritual growth. I know many Christians who have a hard time being gut-honest with God—and I used to be one of them. I tried to hide my sin, hurt and anger. I didn't want to discuss any of it with him and hoped that if I didn't talk to him, he wouldn't notice and my issues would just go away. Who was I kidding? Only myself. I finally accepted that I can't hide anything from God. I came to find comfort in the realization that he wants me to be honest. Now I know he can handle whatever I need to share or confess.

THE LORD UNDERSTANDS

On that Fourth of July afternoon riding with the "sparklers" in the car, I emotionally and mentally flung myself upon Jesus. I told him that he was my best friend. And I didn't feel alone any longer.

The Lord understands our journey as single women. Psalm 42:5-6 helps me realize this. "Why am I discouraged? Why so sad? I will put my hope in God! I will praise him again—my Savior and my God! Now I am deeply discouraged, but I will remember your kindness" (NLT). Thank God that he makes room for us to be honest. This is just one of many Scripture passages that remind us to hold on to Jesus and find comfort in him.

Psalm 139:5 tells us that God places his hand of blessing on our heads (NLT). But do we recognize his hand of blessing? Trusting God's goodness can be difficult. Surely if he knew me, we say, he would know I don't want to stay single the rest of my life. If he were as loving and concerned as he says he is, he would guide us to the person we want to be with. He would give us freedom to choose our own way.

The issue of singleness and marriage is big enough to make or break our faith. We find it difficult to accept that we're precious to God when he doesn't give us what we think we need. We find that our will collides with God's. But God has planned our lives carefully and intimately. Are we willing to surrender our will to his? Even though we wrestle, it's possible to come to appreciate God's will and presence in our lives, and to find that Abba knows best.

FOR BETTER OR FOR WORSE

You've heard it recited at dozens of weddings, but the phrase "for

---

HOLDING ON TO JESUS

In Psalm 139:3, we see God's awareness of our lives and his activity in it. "You chart the path ahead of me and tell me where to stop and rest. Every moment you know where I am" (NLT). God does chart the path ahead of us, although we may feel sometimes that he's charted the wrong path. If we were honest, what path would we suggest to him? Something radically different? The psalmist says God tells us where to stop and rest; are they the same places we would choose? Probably not—at least not all the time. However, if we were to chart our own path, we would find no real rest. True rest and peace are found only in the center of his will. He precedes and follows his children. He is the only wise God.

better or for worse" also applies to the single life. Instead of choosing a man, we're choosing an outlook on life. We're declaring that no one is responsible for our contentment but us and God. Blaming others for our circumstances may seem easier, but it doesn't lead anywhere except to further discontentment. My cooperation with God, or lack thereof, determines how I see life. If I have a positive perspective on singleness, I probably have a positive view of life and God. And vice versa.

In 1981, Barbara went to Pakistan as a missionary. After language study, she worked as a nurse-midwife at a hospital for Pakistani women and children and lived in a bungalow for single women on the hospital compound. A friend of Barbara's suggested that I interview her for a view of singleness as a missionary. I chose to do just that! She states,

> The missionary community became my family away from home. They were the people I lived with, socialized with and worked with on a daily basis. In some ways, that was the most satisfying and fulfilling period of my life. But there were also times when I was terribly lonely, either because friendship was not reciprocated or because of criticism from my colleagues. I left in 1989 for an extended furlough and did not return long-term.

For Barbara, singleness made it easy to pick up and move to various places and afforded opportunities for ministry. Recently, it allowed her to move closer to her aging parents. She continues,

> In each of these moves I believed God was calling me. I was making my career a priority, although I imagined and hoped early on that marriage would happen, perhaps with a doctor on the field or someone involved in ministry where I was. There have been times over the years when I have longed for the intimacy I saw in a few married couples around me.

I can't really see myself married now. That's partly because I can't imagine a man being interested in me at this point, and also because I would have reservations about sharing my assets—unless, of course, he was bringing more assets into the relationship than I was! It would be hard to adjust my schedule and habits after all these years of living on my own.

Barbara is now fifty-two and lives in the States. She continues to work with the same mission agency as an area mobilizer, informing and raising up more laborers for the harvest. She also works part time as a labor and delivery nurse. For better or for worse.

All of the following questions have come to mind at one time or another in my single life as I have tried to live for better or for worse, and many of them may sound familiar to you too. How would you answer them?

- How can I be patient when it seems everyone around me is finding the love of their life?
- How do I make the most of my time and not get distracted?
- How can I better focus on God and serve others?
- How do I deal with friends who are not comfortable in their singleness, those who believe their worth is tied to their marital status?
- How can I stay positive and focused when others around me are negative?

We're going to talk about all this and more in the rest of this book. My prayer is that as you read, you will ask yourself what God wants of you in your life right now. Not in five or ten years, when you see yourself married with two kids, but right now. Are you willing to follow him no matter what?

THE CHALLENGE OF WAITING

Sometimes we're tempted to think that God is forcing us to play the waiting game while he takes bets on how we'll hold up. And the odds don't seem to be in our favor—it's a couples' world and society tells us that happiness is impossible unless we're paired up. Unfortunately, Christians have bought into this lie. But does the God we know really toy with us for his own amusement?

Some people do walk away from God when they don't find a mate. Disappointment sets in and they find it too difficult to trust his goodness. Rather than acknowledging that he knows what's best for their life, they blame him for their circumstances. They know he could make it different, and when he doesn't, they abandon their faith and their values. I admit that waiting on God is one of the hardest disciplines we face as Christians. Deep within we know God will fulfill our desires and needs, but when his timetable seems off, it's a challenge to keep believing. Yet as we learn to wait on him and trust him, we learn more about his character and discover that his tender care wants only our best, even if that best differs dramatically from what we want.

Our goal is to find contentment in God alone. If we learn to wait on him rather than the perfect husband, we'll experience contentment much sooner. The fact is, not everyone will marry. And if we force the issue, if we're determined to have a boyfriend or mate regardless of what God thinks, we're asking for a whole mess of trouble and turmoil. I've seen it countless times and I'm sure you have too. Consider these questions:

- In what ways are you trying to win the waiting game?
- What is your attitude toward God as you wait?
- What do you need from God in order to better trust his timing?
- How can God help you become more content?

When we share our honest feelings with God, he will help us find contentment in him first. If we aren't careful, our lives will pass us by and we will miss cultivating our love-relationship with God. We will wake up at the end of our lives and wonder what it was all about. We will realize how much time we wasted on earthly versus eternal things. Let's wake up before then—right now—while we can still do something about it!

SINGLENESS: A BLESSING

It may not feel like it when your best friend rides off in the limo after her wedding reception, or when your back is killing you from sleeping on the couch at your brother and sister-in-law's house, but singleness is actually a blessing. "Yeah, right," I can hear you saying. "And how's that?" Here's the key: singleness is a blessing because it gives us the opportunity to trust that God desires our very best. And in order to trust God, we must come to know this loving God intimately—an incredible blessing.

How we view our singleness hinges on how completely we give our plans, ambitions and desires into God's hands. In my small group, the word *surrender* comes up a lot. We discuss what we think surrender is and is not. We've mostly concluded that surrender is hard. It's tough to give ourselves over totally to someone we can't see. We read about God in his Word and believe Scripture to be true, but trusting him implicitly is quite another thing.

I've found that the key to trust is love. If I know someone loves me, I'm more prone to trust him or her. For a long time I knew in my head that God loved me, but I didn't feel that love consistently. So I was moody. My happiness and joy were circumstantial. One day I cried out to God and asked him to help me feel his love. Then I started looking for him to do so. Scales seemed to fall from my eyes as I became more and more aware of his numerous, often minute-by-minute expressions of tenderness for me. Now I keep a journal to record the occasions when God has used others' words to encourage me. I also keep boxes of cards and notes to re-read when I need an emotional boost. Daily I am more aware of God's infinite love for me.

Singleness is a blessing when we know the peace of God, which also comes from trusting him. Philippians 4:6-7 tells us to "be anxious for nothing, but in everything by prayer and supplication with thanksgiving let your requests be made known to God. And the peace of God, which surpasses all comprehension, will guard your hearts and your minds in Christ Jesus." When we let go and relax, knowing he is God, we can be at peace.

Peace also results from an intimate relationship with the Father. In Psalm 46:10 we're told to be still and know that he is God (NIV). But we find it extremely difficult to be still, don't we? The enemy has fed us a line that to be busy is to be godly. He tells us we should scurry around in the name of God and leave no time available to relate with our Father personally. We may even think that if we're busy for him he'll give us what we want. I've often wondered what God's face looks like as he watches his children industriously trying to do his work without his constant guidance and strength. Our priorities, desires and needs get all mixed up when we're not relating intimately with God—and peace eludes us.

If you are a single adult woman struggling to find contentment, my prayer is that one day you will know this truth. I pray that you will know God's love for you. I pray that you will experience his peace that surpasses all comprehension, regardless of your circumstances. I pray that you will be a witness to the world around you that God is trustworthy. I pray that you will know a contented heart, one that waits for God's best. I pray that you won't live another day questioning God's goodness because you don't have a boyfriend or a mate. In the meantime, I pray that if God desires marriage for you, you're prepared to be the best spouse possible to the glory of God.

QUESTIONS FOR REFLECTION OR DISCUSSION

1. Have you ever had an experience similar to the July Fourth parade story? If so, how did it make you feel?

2. How would you respond to the statement "Singleness is a curse"?

3. What comes to your mind when you think of "for better or for worse" as a single adult?

4. As a single adult, in what ways do you feel accepted? Not accepted?

5. Do you believe we live in a couples-oriented society? If so, how does it affect you?

6. Describe your level of contentment as a single Christian adult. How would you change it?

7. Do you view singleness as a blessing? Why or why not?

Enjoying the Benefits of Single Life

Sometimes it seems that people think I have the plague because I'm single and I love it. When I told my coworker Sherry that I heard God's call to singleness when I was thirty, she screamed and said, "No!" I could see that she thought the condition might be contagious. You see, Sherry is single; she can hardly bear the thought that God might ask her to remain that way.

I'm not saying it's always easy. I've often felt alone at church. In the past I dreaded the end of the service when families and couples would leave together, chatting happily, as I left alone. At times I would walk out hurriedly, eyes fixed straight ahead so I wouldn't notice those around me and they wouldn't see my jealousy and hurt. Other times I would take my time, perusing the room to see if I could connect with a friend or ask someone to lunch. Sometimes it worked and I would fellowship with other believers, but just as often I still left without having had a meaningful conversation. Soon, however, I began to see that God wanted me to trust him to put people into my life.

Over a period of several years, God's invitation to walk in single-ness became a deep desire. And as I've walked with him in obedience, I've become more aware of the benefits of this lifestyle. My intimacy with God has grown along with my desire for singleness.

THE DIFFICULT BUT REWARDING PATH TO GROWTH

I have longed to know what it means for God to be my everything, and as I mature I'm finding out what that's like. Let me tell you, it's glorious. God's Word is a significant avenue of growth. As I pore over Scripture, I come to know both God and myself more fully.

I'm thankful that I started keeping a diary in junior high. I've scribbled my feelings and thoughts over the pages of many note-books since then. Through the years my journal has reflected not so much the events of my life but my walk with the Lord. I commune with him in prayer, worshiping and pouring out my heart before him. This time alone with God in his Word and in my journal is my primary source of developing intimacy with him.

My intimacy with God has also developed through fellowship with like-minded Christians. For example, one day I was out shopping and a clerk named Melody approached me with a bright smile. She spent a lot of time helping me find just what I was looking for. As I talked about my life in Jesus, she shared about him too. Before I left, I asked her if she was a Christian. She said, "Yes, and I'm thankful that I am." I said, "I wondered; you speak the language." I share what God is doing in my life within my circle of close friends as well, and they do the same. We pray for one another with expectation that he will answer our prayers. I'm thankful for their encouragement to keep pressing on to honor the Lord.

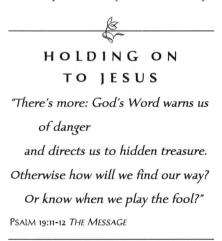

HOLDING ON TO JESUS

"There's more: God's Word warns us of danger

and directs us to hidden treasure.

Otherwise how will we find our way?

Or know when we play the fool?"

PSALM 19:11-12 *THE MESSAGE*

Though I'm certainly still growing, I've come a long way from the days of being uncomfortable in church. Corporate worship now encourages me to pursue God as we sing and hear God's Word proclaimed instead of making me painfully aware of my single status. As I learn to be aware of God's presence, I see him working in my life and all around me, giving me opportunities to reach out and care for others and allowing them to do the same for me.

I haven't always found it easy to receive others' care. I used to focus so much on others that I neglected myself, and the more exhausted I became, the more my intimacy with God suffered. Joining the staff of InterVarsity and raising my financial support rocked my illusion of self-sufficiency in a big way. I had no choice but to receive from others. I was humbled and stretched as I asked people to consider supporting me—and finances were just part of it. I needed prayer and friendship as much as money, and my support team rose to the occasion. Then and now they have given of themselves in innumerable ways. And I am grateful.

My growth has also come about through caring for others, and I thank God for giving that privilege. Shortly after starting a new job, two of my new coworkers poured out their hearts to me. They knew I was in Christian ministry and felt comfortable enough to ask questions and share with me. I was moved with compassion as I listened and responded. To this day I believe the primary reason I went to work that day was for the sake of those two coworkers. The honor of being used by God in this way is both gratifying and humbling.

WHAT'S SO GREAT ABOUT BEING SINGLE?

Singleness is God's idea. If you're unmarried you're free to care about the concerns of the Lord and how to please him. If you're married, your interests are divided. You have to pay attention to worldly things in order to support your family and focus on pleasing your spouse (1 Corinthians 7:32-34). Now obviously, marriage is also part of God's plan. But the apostle Paul emphasizes the value of singleness: "This I say for your own benefit; not to put a restraint upon you, but to promote what is appropriate and to secure undistracted devotion to the Lord" (1 Corinthians 7:35).

The primary benefit of being single is to have the opportunity for undistracted devotion to the Lord. But even without a husband and children, maintaining our focus on him is a never-ending challenge. Things and people are constantly competing for our devotion, and the battle can be fierce. The enemy loves to distract us from following Christ wholeheartedly. We need to stay aware of his tactics. He may silently whisper to us, *Jesus is not enough; he can't meet your every need.* Or, *You're too busy for a quiet time right now.* Or, *It's OK to be in this relationship with Jeremy even though he's not a Christian. God just doesn't understand; you need to have your needs met.*

The crucial question is, Is Jesus enough? Can the one who made us, entirely fulfill us? If we were to be gut-honest, would we say that Jesus satisfies us on all levels? Emotionally? Men-

HOLDING ON TO JESUS

"The revelation of GOD is whole

and pulls our lives together.

The signposts of GOD are clear

and point out the right road.

The life-maps of GOD are right,

showing the way to joy.

The directions of GOD are plain

and easy on the eyes."

PSALM 19:7-8, THE MESSAGE

tally? Physically? Spiritually? To enjoy the benefits of singleness to the limits of what's possible, we must answer these questions. Our lives give evidence as to what we really believe.

How we answer the question "Is Jesus enough?" affects our whole belief system. If Jesus is enough, he will provide our every need, though his ideas about what we need may differ significantly from ours. The question "Is Jesus enough?" raises other questions, such as:

- How aligned is my will with God's?
- Do I really believe he knows what's best for me?
- Could he really think a life of singleness is for my best?
- Can I trust him?
- Will I trust him whether I feel my needs are met or not?

Fortunately, God is gracious to meet us right where we are, in the midst of our frustrations, questions and joys.

In interviewing people for this book, I asked them what they saw as the greatest benefit of singleness. The overwhelming response was, "Time to do as I please, with no restrictions or need to get permission from a spouse." God gives us the gift of time. We can use it to worship him, grow and invest in the lives of others. Or we can chase after phantoms that promise fulfillment but lead only to frustration and emptiness. Nothing reveals our priorities like how we use our time. Heather says this:

> Singleness has been a gift to me. It has been a time for me to run wholeheartedly after God. Nothing hinders me from spending lots of time studying his Word, praying, journaling, meditating and memorizing Scriptures. Also, I'm free to invest in the lives of others. I've been able to go to several other countries and disciple younger women, be involved with a pregnancy crisis center, work on my master's in biblical counseling and volunteer with the homeless.

That's a woman who knows how to use her time. She continues,

> Singleness helps me get to know who God created me to be. I can freely dream and explore what ministries I thrive in the most. The most important lesson I've learned as a single adult is contentment with God, today. He is enough for me, and he gives me what he wants me to have today. I can wish today away

and hope for something more, or I can live today as if it were my last—fully to the glory of God, loving him and loving whoever he has placed in my life. My hope must rest in Christ because I am not guaranteed that I will be married or have anything other than what I have today. I trust that God uses every day to prepare me for what's to come, and only he knows what that is.

Other observations on the benefits of singleness cover everything from the freedom to spend money as desired to the absence of arguments in decision-making. Here are a few comments from some of your fellow single sisters:

- "I can watch whatever TV show I want and listen to whatever music I desire."
- "I don't have to cook or clean house if I don't want to."
- "I don't have to try to please someone all the time."
- "I have my own ideas. It seems to me that some married women repress their ideas and opinions in deference to their husband's perspectives."

The word *freedom* encapsulates these comments and expresses much of what I enjoy about singleness. Mary Ann, another single Christian woman, agrees:

I hugely enjoy being single, and I'm grateful to have entered my thirties without getting married. Staying single this long has given me more freedom to explore my identity and find my calling. I've entered and left grad school, moved around a lot and learned internal strength and survival skills. I can do this more readily because I'm not having to negotiate with someone else about where we'll live and how we'll spend our time. These are solely my decisions. I also appreciate how singleness gives me freedom to be radical. I'm currently pursuing downward mobility—selling my possessions, refusing to own a car or a TV—and this could be harder if I were married.

Mary Ann also appreciates the way singleness gives her greater independence and flexibility. She continues,

> I can follow my own schedule, eating when I'm hungry, carrying on with a project if I'm deeply into it, reading in bed without worrying that the light will keep my partner awake. I have more free time to devote to what I like to do, whether that's ministries or hobbies or building friendships. I have more space in my heart (as well as my schedule) to give to an array of people and causes, and to get the alone time I need. My time with God is expansive and intimate, and I've learned to lean heavily into his arms.

Freedom, sweet freedom. The thought of it repulses some and encourages others.

THE CHOICE IS YOURS

If we live out these benefits, we as single adults can take the lead in demonstrating a Christian lifestyle of worship. My aunt Florrie, a widow for many years, exemplifies worshiping God as a way of life. Soon into a conversation with her you will probably hear her say, "The Lord is so good, he is just so good, and I praise him for his goodness to me."

But even better than contemporary role models are the examples we find in Scripture. The apostle Paul was undistracted in his devotion to the Lord. He knew the value of remaining focused on God and was willing to pay any price to maintain that focus. While we're constantly facing insinuations that we should marry, Paul exhorts us to remain single and give Jesus our all. Speaking of Jesus, his life also demonstrates unswerving devotion to the Father. Jesus looked to see what his heavenly Father was doing so he could join him. "I can do nothing on My own initiative," Jesus says in John 5:30. He left an example of God-centeredness for us.

What are we doing with the single life God has given us? Are we using it for his glory and our good, or are we squandering it? Are we willing to align our will with his? If we're enjoying our singleness, let's rejoice. If we're not, we need to go humbly before God and state our cause. We can express our feelings, whatever they are—anger, hurt, disappointment or loneliness. Remember, he wants our honesty. He can handle it and will meet us there. Two Scriptures promise this:

> Therefore humble yourselves under the mighty hand of God, that He may exalt you at the proper time, casting all your anxiety on Him, because He cares for you. (1 Peter 5:6-7)

> The path of the righteous is like the light of dawn,
> That shines brighter and brighter until the full day. (Proverbs 4:18)

May our paths shine brighter and brighter like the light of dawn until we see our Savior face to face.

QUESTIONS FOR REFLECTION OR DISCUSSION

1. As a single adult, in what ways do you demonstrate undistracted devotion to the Lord?
2. Do you believe Jesus is enough to meet your every need? Why or why not?
3. What suggestions would you give in caring for the things of the Lord?
4. Give examples of how your life is pleasing to the Lord.
5. How would you evaluate your single status at this time in your life?

Listening to God

Eighteen years ago I heard a quiet voice within ask, *What if I never want you to marry?*

Where is this question coming from? I asked myself. I took my question to God. *Is it you speaking?* I asked. As I prayed, a strong *yes* permeated my heart. Now God was waiting for my response. I prayed some more, then answered, *If that's what you want, Lord, then that's what I want also.*

Several weeks later I realized that if I remained single, I would never bear my own children, a reality I had not factored into my answer. I came to God with my concern, and he gave me peace that even this was OK. I could trust him. Once again I said, *Yes*.

I struggled to make sense of these conversations with God. I wanted to talk about my thoughts and feelings with someone. But after sharing with one or two people, I felt frustrated. No one seemed to understand. Words from my journal capture my frustration.

Young, Black, Christian, thirty-year-old single woman—that's me. Why are people challenging who I am? Why are people trying to make me someone else, make me uncomfortable in who I am? Many reasons, I guess. Tonight I tried not to feel attacked because I'm single and male relationships are not a priority. I cannot allow others to define who I am. Why can't I just be me without unnecessary judgments? Leave me alone. I'm glad there's you, Jesus. I'm comfortable with you. Thanks for being with me.

With those words I committed myself to God's will.

In further response to God, I asked him to make me aware of his presence. Accepting a lifestyle of singleness necessitated an intimate walk with him. Now more than ever I needed to know he was close by. He needed to show me how to depend on him in new and deeper ways. After praying this prayer, my spiritual antennas were on high alert for signals of his presence and love.

HEARING GOD'S VOICE

I'm often asked how I heard God's call to be single. That question is generally followed by the comment, "I hope I don't hear it!" But the greater question is, How do we hear God at all?

Learning to hear from God means listening for him in every area of our lives. Trusting God with our marital status challenges and sometimes almost silences our relationship with him. If he doesn't give us what we want when we want it, our faith may land on shaky ground.

I think of my friend Jennifer, who walked away from her faith because God hadn't given her a husband. Disappointed, she shared, "I've been walking with him and serving him, and he hasn't given me a man." According to Jennifer, God hadn't held up his end of the bargain. I lost touch with her but recently ran into a mutual friend. I asked about Jennifer and learned some sad news: she had left the church and was living with her boyfriend.

Even when God seems far away and his will cloudy and confusing, we can be confident that he will speak to us. He won't leave us in the dark; he's promised us that. Still, you may say, it's hard to listen to God. I agree. When he doesn't respond to our desires the way we want him to, it's hard to believe he really cares about us. When we see others around us getting what they want (e.g., a man), we may wonder what's wrong with us. When we've been faithful in serving God, it's hard to accept that he won't grant us such a deep desire as marriage. And yet throughout Scripture, God asks us to listen to him. Regardless.

HOLDING ON TO JESUS

"Therefore the LORD longs to be

gracious to you,

And therefore He waits on high to

have compassion on you.

For the LORD is a God of justice;

How blessed are all those who long

for Him."

ISAIAH 30:18

HEARING AND RESPONDING TO GOD

The plea of God in Psalm 81:8-16 penetrates my heart every time I read it. And when I read the entire psalm, I see why God admonishes us to listen to and obey him. This passage even speaks to us about how to live as single women, with radical devotion to the Lord. Listen closely to the psalmist's words.

Sing for joy to God our strength;
    Shout joyfully to the God of Jacob.
    Raise a song, strike the timbrel,
    The sweet sounding lyre with the harp.
    Blow the trumpet at the new moon,
    At the full moon, on our feast day. (Psalm 81:1-3)

The psalmist begins by telling Israel how to praise God. We may not strike a timbrel, play a harp or blow a trumpet, but we can praise God in our own ways. What gets your blood pumping with praise? Music? Singing and playing instruments have been used to praise

God since Bible times. So has dancing, so get out there and shake it
if doing so helps you worship (and the situation is appropriate!). In
more contemplative moments, we can focus on his attributes with
adoration, joy and gratitude.

> For it is a statute for Israel,
> An ordinance of the God of Jacob.
> He established it for a testimony in Joseph
> When he went throughout the land of Egypt.
> I heard a language that I did not know. (Psalm 81:4-5)

Worship was a law for Israel to give testimony of God's faithfulness. Through praise they remembered how he had rescued them
from Egypt. He demonstrated his faithfulness to them even when
they couldn't understand, when Israel "heard a language that I did
not know." Like Israel, we acknowledge God's faithfulness to us when
we worship, even when we can't understand what he's doing and why
he makes certain choices for our lives.

> I relieved his shoulder of the burden,
> His hands were freed from the basket.
> You called in trouble and I rescued you;
> I answered you in the hiding place of thunder;
> I proved you at the waters of Meribah. Selah.
> (Psalm 81:6-7)

Here the psalmist gives details of how God rescued Israel. Their
burdens were lifted and their hands freed from slavery. The people
cried out in the midst of their toil and strain, and God answered.
Then he tested Israel's faithfulness. Does this sound familiar? When
has God lifted your burdens and freed you? Have you ever cried out
to him in the midst of your storms and received his answer? Remember those times—it's so easy to forget. If you feel you're being tested,
remember his faithfulness with praise.

> Hear, O My people, and I will admonish you;
> O Israel, if you would listen to Me! (Psalm 81:8)

In this verse God is pleading for Israel to listen to him. He knows the disaster they're headed for apart from him and longs to keep them safe by his side. He does the same with us. He wants to protect us from our own bad decisions. As you examine your life and take time to listen to God, especially in regard to your singleness, is it possible that he's warning you against something that will only end in pain and heartache? Can you hear his voice of admonition?

> Let there be no strange god among you;
> Nor shall you worship any foreign god. (Psalm 81:9)

Like Israel, we are tempted to follow other gods, something God indicates over and over again throughout Scripture that he will not tolerate. As single adults, we may make other gods out of relationships. Desperation for companionship with the opposite sex overrides our desire for God's best, and when we're called to relinquish this false god, it rips at the core of who we are. Raise your hand if you've been there. Maybe eventually we'll learn not to stray from the true God.

> I, the LORD, am your God,
> Who brought you up from the land of Egypt;
> Open your mouth wide and I will fill it. (Psalm 81:10)

The Lord is our God. We belong to him and we're his family. As he brought Israel out from the land of Egypt, he brings us out from our Egypts, from our own forms of slavery. He fills and satisfies us. In realizing this truth, we have to wrestle with our ability to trust him to provide our best. We wrestle as Jacob did, coming to realize our need for God and his intervention right smack in the middle of our desires.

But My people did not listen to My voice,
And Israel did not obey Me.
So I gave them over to the stubbornness of their heart,
To walk in their own devices. (Psalm 81:11-12)

Here's the bottom line: When Israel didn't listen to God or obey him, it did not go well for them. They were ultimately defeated by their enemies and exiled. God in his mercy later restored them. Anytime we refuse to heed God's voice, we put ourselves on a downward spiral in life. Although we may think we're doing well, we're not. We often walk through many unnecessary trials to finally realize how mistaken we have been.

Oh that My people would listen to Me,
That Israel would walk in My ways!
I would quickly subdue their enemies
And turn My hand against their adversaries. (Psalm 81:13-14)

I marvel at God's patience. I would have thrown up my hands and given up on these people a long time ago. But thank God for his compassion, which he displays toward us as well. He wants to fight for us and show himself strong on our behalf—if only we would listen to him. In listening to and obeying God, we keep ourselves under the umbrella of his care. No, he never leaves or forsakes his children, but he does sometimes let us learn from our stubbornness.

Those who hate the LORD would pretend obedience to Him,
And their time of punishment would be forever. (Psalm 81:15)

People who pretend obedience to the Lord and never repent perish forever. And sometimes as believers we pretend obedience, forgetting that God sees and knows everything. We go to church and Bible study, talking the talk of the spiritual life, when in our hearts we're harboring sin we know God wants us to give up. We're very good at keeping up appearances. The Hebrew word for "pretend," *kachash*, means "to disappoint, deceive, fail and grow lean." Anytime we pretend obedience we disappoint ourselves, even though we may not recognize it right away. We also deceive ourselves into thinking we're going the right way when in our hearts we know we're not. And then when we fail, often we blame God first. Again, thank God for his mercy, which is demonstrated in the next verse.

But I would feed you with the finest of the wheat,
And with honey from the rock I would satisfy you.
(Psalm 81:16)

In essence, this psalm tells us we need to be relieved, freed, rescued, answered, fed and satisfied. And when we look for anyone or anything else to do this for us, we get into trouble—deep trouble of the soul. God created us to need and desire him first and foremost; this is worship. Through this love relationship with him, he fills and satisfies us. He transforms our desires into his, which leads to a deeper joy than anything offered by this early life.

LISTENING AND WORSHIP

If you are a woman who wants to marry and who has waited a long time, Jesus wants to commune with you, wants you to hear his voice, wants you to know that right now he is enough. He longs to comfort and encourage you. When he is at the center of our affection and adoration, we're in a position to hear him. When we're quiet long enough to reflect upon our lives in his presence, we're more apt to live satisfied lives. God meets every single woman where she is and desires to show himself in mighty ways. It is in communing with him that life makes sense. In these moments of intimate fellowship with him, we worship.

Worship pastor Rick Cobb says, "Worship is communication and response. God communicates and we respond." In this process we move into what he called, in a prepared message, the rhythm of worship.

We acknowledge. Worship always begins with an acknowledgement of who God is. We acknowledge and declare the personhood of God. We publicize his revealed nature, works, promises and will for our lives. "In all your ways acknowledge Him" (Proverbs 3:6).

We cease. Because of the society that we live in and the frantic pace that we keep, we cease from our efforts to be in control of our own lives. "Be still, and know that I am God" (Psalm 46:10 NIV).

We rest. We rest in the presence and the provision of the Lord. "Come to Me, all who are weary and heavy-laden, and I will give you rest. Take My yoke upon you and learn from Me, for I am gentle and humble in heart, and you will find rest for your souls" (Matthew 11:28-29).

We listen. We listen as God speaks to us through his Word and as we worship. "I will hear what God the LORD will say" (Psalm 85:8).

We respond. We respond with an obedient heart to what God is saying and doing. We realize that God's intentions for his people have always been for the whole person to respond. "But the word is very near you, in your mouth and in your heart, that you may observe it" (Deuteronomy 30:14).

To this list to I would add confession. Confession cleans the slate between us and God, restoring our souls. By it we are consistently reminded of God's forgiveness. I've clung to 1 John 1:9 for many years now: "If we confess our sins, He is faithful and righteous to forgive us our sins and to cleanse us from all unrighteousness."

GETTING OUR ATTENTION

Because God is faithful, he uses many avenues to get our attention. He uses his people, prayer, his Word, impressions or ideas from the Holy Spirit, circumstances, service, nature, imagination and even silence. My friend Joyce, who's been single again for four years now, has been comforted, challenged and guided as God has spoken to her in numerous ways in this season of her life. One way he does this is through books. Joyce loves to read and is open to learning from Christian authors. God also used a counselor to help her deal with painful issues in her life.

When Joyce received training as a prayer counselor to help others get through their trials, she was helped herself. She recognized a gap in her walk with the Lord, areas that needed healing. While I was visiting Joyce once, she showed me her garden. She stated, "Gardening does me good; immersing myself in growing things calms me." As she focuses on the beauty of nature in her garden and the tender care it needs, she's reminded of the need to

---

HOLDING ON TO JESUS

Do we know what it means to be content? Philippians 4:11-13 describes it: "Not that I speak from want, for I have learned to be content in whatever circumstances I am. I know how to get along with humble means, and I also know how to live in prosperity; in any and every circumstance I have learned the secret of being filled and going hungry, both of having abundance and suffering need. I can do all things through Him who strengthens me." This passage can apply to any of our needs. God knows whether we are physically, mentally, emotionally or spiritually empty, and he will fill us up accordingly.

---

focus on her relationship with Christ, remembering she can't rescue or fix anybody else by herself. God is communicating with Joyce in ways that speak to her soul most intimately. She keeps herself open to him, not stepping ahead or looking for someone else to meet her needs.

In response to God's caring voice, Joyce thanks him that she is "saved, sane and celibate." She says, "He's showed me how to walk this path through worship, studying his Word, and understanding the timetable of history. I love to study prophecy. It helps me to remember that we're passing through. I listen to him to get his perspective so that I can be at peace with his will."

Is It Really You, God?

The Phillips translation of John 14:26 reads, "The Holy Spirit . . . will be your teacher and will bring to your mind all I have said to you." When listening for God to speak through impressions and ideas from the Holy Spirit, we need to confirm what we're hearing by comparing it to biblical teaching. A speaker I once heard said that when the Holy Spirit brings something to mind, it's inspiration. When the devil brings something to mind, it's temptation. I've experienced this truth. When I have a thought that seems to come from God, I examine it closely. I pray and ask the Holy Spirit to confirm it. I put it alongside the Word of God to make sure it matches up. I examine it to see if it fits God's character and sounds like something he would say— specifically something he would say to me. Sometimes I seek counsel from a trusted friend. I look for peace and persistence in my heart. If I get a green light on all of the above, I move ahead.

Sometimes it's just a gentle nudge from the Spirit and I don't understand it at all. For instance, one night at the residential treatment center where I work, I saw another staff member sitting alone taking her break. I had met her only briefly one time, so I didn't know her very well. But as I passed by where she was sitting, I felt a nudge to go and talk with her. I didn't want to, and I almost dismissed the impulse. But I've learned that you don't say no to the Holy Spirit. So I thought, "Oh well, I might as well say hello."

I struck up a conversation with the woman, whose name was Alice. Shortly into the conversation, she started to reveal some personal struggles she was experiencing in her life. I shared with her how Christ had helped me in my difficult times, and by the end of the conversation Alice had agreed to do a Bible study with me. In our first session, she gave her life to Christ. Yay, God! I was ecstatic. We're still meeting to go through the basics of Christianity, and Alice's growth has been steady. We've agreed that that first conversation was divinely appointed, and I'm so thankful I heeded that gentle nudge.

I've heard people say that they're not sure when it's God they're hearing. It does take time to learn to recognize the Spirit's voice, but it's truly worth the effort. Testing our thoughts and impulses against God's Word, seeking input from mature Christians, and looking for confirmation within our spirit are all ways to build this discipline. The more we honestly try to heed God's voice, the better equipped we will be to hear him. Bill Hybels offers additional insight in his book *Too Busy Not to Pray*:

> Question the leading if it requires making a major, life-changing decision in a short period of time. Take precaution if the leading requires going deeply into debt or placing someone else in a position of awkwardness, compromise or danger. Beware if the leading requires shattering family relationships or important friendships. Continue to pray for clarity if the leading creates unrest in the spirit of a mature Christian friend or counselor as you share it with them.

Is This the One?

God is committed to communicating with us even when he must speak a hard word, because he knows his purpose for us. Learning to trust his voice and goodness requires lifelong training. Matthew 7:9-11 demonstrates this truth: "What man is there among you who, when his son asks for a loaf, will give him a stone? Or if he asks for a fish, he will not give him a snake, will he? If you then, being evil, know how to give good gifts to your children, how much more will your Father who is in heaven give what is good to those who ask Him!"

My friend Leah has found this to be true in her dating life. Here's her story in her words.

> When I first met John, I thought, what a neat guy. He seemed different from most godly men I'd known, with an incredible heart and passion for God. Each time he came into my workplace we had a short conversation. He treated me to dinner one evening, and as I sat there listening I couldn't help but think, "Is this guy for real?" He seemed too big for life.
>
> As time went on, he started to call me at work quite often. One day he asked if he could cook dinner for me, and he prepared a delicious meal. The evening turned out to be the most fun I'd ever had on a date. I felt comfortable with him.
>
> Weeks later I was planning a dinner for friends. He seemed interested in coming and I knew he hadn't socialized in a while, so I invited him. Two things stood out to me that night. One, he treated me like a queen, and two, he bragged about himself the whole time! All he did was talk about himself and his intimate relationship with the Father. Who did he think he was—better than everybody else? Didn't he think other people might have the same relationship with the Father? His bragging made me furious.
>
> I kept my distance for the next month. But the desire for a relationship grew. During that time John started working some in our office. I asked myself where my desire came from—God

or my flesh? As we continued to talk, I fought the relationship. I cried out to God for release. But one day John came into the office and looked sad, saying he'd had a hard weekend. I told him I hoped we were good enough friends that he could share with me. That really got the ball rolling.

I kept the relationship secret for two months. I finally decided to tell some close friends because I wanted their wisdom and input. One friend responded that she saw John as a counterfeit, that he wasn't God's best for me. Although I didn't want to admit it, that statement lingered in the back of my mind.

The relationship grew and we started to spend almost every day together. But at the same time I started to feel pressure to end it. I wanted to get away from John but didn't know how. A war raged inside of me. I remained confused, wanting to be with him and not wanting to be with him at the same time.

One night at my home we watched a movie lying on the couch. Big mistake! He started kissing me when I turned toward him, and the physical closeness escalated. Fortunately, I burst into tears and stopped it before it progressed any further. He said we had done nothing wrong. He justified our physical behavior. As I saw it, I violated him and he violated me. I realized then we were not on the same page.

I called two close friends the next night and cried on the phone. John and I had never discussed physical boundaries. I'd hoped he would take the leadership in that area. After receiving counsel from my friends, looking honestly at the relationship and praying, I found the strength to walk away from John.

Leah admits she made mistakes throughout this relationship. Red flags were all over the place, but in her desire for the relationship to work, she ignored them. John's self-absorption, her desire for secrecy about the relationship and warnings from close friends all should have clued her in that something wasn't right. But instead she proceeded and faced fierce temptation and a difficult internal battle without support or accountability. In the end, though, God saw her through once she turned toward him instead of away.

Although it's hard now when Leah sees John at work, she continues to develop her intimate walk with God. Step by step, she's learning to trust him, and he is leading her to a deeper level of fellowship with himself. Leah is thankful for God's love and patience, and she's grateful for the lessons learned—lessons she hopes she doesn't have to repeat.

A Voice of Comfort

Sometimes God speaks through other people. My new friend Sherry lost her husband to illness, but she carries in her heart the words he spoke on his deathbed. He said to her, "When I have gone home to be with my precious Lord, know that your life will just begin. You can't even begin to imagine the things he has in store for you, honey. And know this, he has someone for you. You will not be alone. You will marry again."

Sherry goes on to say, "I've heard these words from my beloved husband whispered in my heart time and time again since he left this earth. The kindness of the Lord to encourage my heart in this way has been the force that has allowed me to wait for the fulfillment. How wonderful to know that the Lord would give me—give any of us—hope for the future. Sometimes he speaks that hope through those he places in our lives, whoever they may be: family, friend, pastor, teacher, even a stranger. God knows the plans he has for us—to give us a future and a hope."

Yes, the Lord does still speak to his people. He wants us to know his will. He doesn't play games with us. The Bible tells us how God longs to be gracious to us (Isaiah 30:18). He says, "You will seek Me and find Me when you search for Me with all your heart" (Jeremiah 29:13). Won't you seek him while he may be found?

QUESTIONS FOR REFLECTION OR DISCUSSION

1. How would you respond to the age-old question, How do I know it's God speaking?

2. Do you feel God is responsible to speak to you when you have no intent to obey him? Why or why not?

3. In Psalm 81:8-16, what indication is there that God communicates with his people?

4. In what ways have you experienced hearing God's voice?

5. What is God saying to you about your singleness? How are you responding to what you're hearing?

6. Which of the suggested modes of hearing God do you most identify with?

7. What is your response to Leah's story? To Sherry's story?

F O U R

Who Am I?

J esus and his disciples left Galilee and went up to the villages
of Caesarea Philippi. As they were walking along, he asked
them, "Who do people say I am?"

"Well," they replied, "some say John the Baptist, some say Eli-
jah, and others say you are one of the other prophets."

Then Jesus asked, "Who do you say I am?"

Peter replied, "You are the Messiah." (Mark 8:27-29 NLT)

Single. Married. Professor. Mother. Writer. CEO. Pastor. Society
loves to label people according to their various roles and positions.
The issue of identity strikes close to the core of our being because it
has to do with our sense of significance and purpose in life. Have you
ever asked yourself, "Who do people say I am?" Or, "Who do I say I
am?" Most importantly, have you asked, "Who does God say I am?"

In the passage above, it wasn't enough for the disciples to know
what others said about Jesus. They needed to know who he really
was in order to understand his mission and their role in it. In the
same way, I can't live my life based on what others think. I must
know, understand and accept myself for who I am—God's special
creation, tailor-made for his glory. My identity is connected to Jesus
because he gives me life. He defines who I am and enables me to fulfill his purpose for me. Throughout Scripture, God tells us who we
are in him.

First of all, God created and designed us. He wove together every thread of our being. According to Psalm 139, we were placed in our mother's womb by his decision, and we are fearfully and wonderfully made (Psalm 139:13-14). Take a moment to reflect on that truth. God is pleased with his creation of us. He saw us before our conception. We were in his mind. He wanted us and therefore created us for a relationship with him. With this relationship in mind, he wrote down the plans he had for us (Psalm 139:16). Then, because of the kind intention of his will, he adopted us as daughters through Jesus, his beloved Son. God planned for our arrival into his family (Ephesians 1:5). And finally, as God's children we have dual citizenship. We live on earth as children of God, and one day we will live in heaven with Christ.

**HOLDING ON
TO JESUS**

"Long ago, even before he made the world, God loved us and chose us in Christ to be holy and without fault in his eyes. . . . And this gave him great pleasure."

EPHESIANS 1:4 NLT

Despite our clear identity as God's children, some people have difficulty viewing God as a father because of a poor relationship with their earthly dads. Marilyn is one such person. "Most of the time I look at God as my Savior and friend rather than as my father," she says. However, Marilyn participated in a study I led on the fatherhood of God, and soon she began to think of him as a caring father, trusting him to know what was best for her from the perspective of a perfect parent.

At the core of our identity as believers is God's love for us. That love drives all other aspects of our relationship with him, and if we don't have a right understanding of it, we won't understand anything else about who we are in him. I find that reading Romans 5:8, which communicates God's love more clearly than almost any other single verse in the Bible, helps me keep life in perspective. "But God demonstrates His own love toward us, in that while we were yet sinners, Christ died for us." When we couldn't have cared less about God, Christ died anyway. Oh, what love! One of Satan's strategies is to try to discourage us by tampering with our assurance of God's love. He whispers things like, "If God really loved you, he wouldn't have allowed *that* to happen." *That* can come in many forms—both situations and people. Being aware of this strategy of Satan's has helped me pull myself out of self-pity many times.

Jude 21 exhorts us to keep ourselves in the love of God. We can do this by

- Guarding our hearts and minds, keeping them full of truth rather than lies.

- Remembering that God always has our best in mind.

- Learning how to accept God's answers of "wait" and "no" when we pray.

- Developing a lifestyle of gratitude for what God has already given us while we wait for him to unfold our lives according to his plan.

- Examining whether we're living life to our full capacity at the moment and not getting so hung up on the future that we miss today.

- Relinquishing our dreams and desires to God for his safekeeping.

- Embracing the truth that we are accepted in the beloved (Ephesians 1:6), even though sometimes it doesn't feel like it.

On our own we're incapable of applying any of these truths to our lives. But the Holy Spirit will teach us what we need to know and enable us to live it. He is our divine helper (John 16:7, 13-14).

AFRICAN AMERICAN

When I ask myself the question, "Who am I?" a significant part of the answer is "African American." As such I remember the days of segregation vividly. I remember signs reading "colored" and "white" for water fountains and bathrooms. I remember separate food counters. I remember going in the back entrance to the doctor's office, while the white people used the front door.

As a child, I watched how my mom lived in a world of segregation, though I didn't know what it was called then. She acted and reacted to her circumstances with dignity, integrity and courage. She would walk through the back door of the doctor's office with her head held high. She made no apologies for living. She had a purpose in life and was determined to fulfill it.

Mom's reaction to segregation had a positive effect on me. Her security and strength as a person helped me attain a sense of security in who I was. She knew segregation was wrong, but she didn't allow it to poison her. I never saw her act hatefully toward white people, but at the same time she was not intimidated by anyone. Her kindness amidst injustice was contagious. Because of her influence I never developed long-term bitterness toward white people.

Like my mother, I also walk with my head held high, proud of the color of my skin. I'm thankful for my African American heritage, especially the closeness of the community I grew up in. Parents trusted each other with their children. If other adults saw me misbehave, they had the authority to discipline me. And when they told my parents about my misbehaving, that usually meant more discipline. My heart remains grateful for this community, for the way people cared for me and poured life into me.

I'm also thankful for the influence of my church growing up. I attended an all-black church into my young adulthood. It was the world I knew, and I felt affirmed and safe in it. My pastor became my spiritual dad. He and his wife invested in me and believed in me. They thought I could make something of myself, and they wanted to play a part in making that happen.

I especially remember the respect given to the elderly. They were venerated pillars of the community, and we didn't talk back to our elders if we knew what was good for us. I have warm memories of numerous family friends who nurtured me. Ms. Lilly Pearl comes to mind. I always felt welcome in her home, and I especially enjoyed going around when she'd made some of those hot apple tarts. She was a gracious and kind woman.

Ms. Estella was my Sunday school teacher in my elementary years. What a jewel. I often think of her now and miss her. She died, according to the way I see it, far too soon. Her faith, gentleness and warm smile soothed my heart—I can still see that smile today. She was the kind of woman you simply wanted to hang out with and get lots of hugs from.

Because I went to college near my hometown, I came home often. I remained active in my community and church. After college I moved four hours away, but I would still come home every four to six weeks to enjoy the comforts of home. It was sad to watch my older friends become more frail. And as they died, the face of the community changed. They were the glue that held us together. I wish the young people of today could have known the older people of my day. They were graced with courage. They were survivors. They were people of integrity. I drew strength from them.

Several years later I moved to the big city and settled down in a community of mixed ethnicity, and I've stayed in that kind of environment to this day. For the first several years I felt like a little black fish out of water—not only because I was living in a large city but also because I wasn't able to connect with home as often. Needless to say, I had large phone bills. These days, although both my parents are dead and many older friends gone, I still go back home. I mostly visit my Aunt Florrie. Once in a while I see the few older friends that remain, and a few of my childhood friends.

As I think of where I came from and the person I am today, I thank

God for his wisdom in placing me in the family, ethnicity and culture he did. Although we may wonder at his choices for our lives sometimes, we can be confident he knows what he's doing. Through the joys and sorrows, he will enable us to emerge as the person he created us to be. Nothing is wasted in our background and history—he uses it all. Praise God for Romans 8:28, which reminds us that he works all things together for good for those who love him and are called according to his purpose.

Even more important to me than my rich African American heritage is my identity in Christ. Apart from him I wouldn't have the first clue about who I am. Left to culture and ethnicity alone, I would be groping in darkness trying to find my way, trying to make sense out of life. He chose my skin color and the circumstances surrounding my birth and childhood. He makes no mistakes.

As you consider your own identity, think about these questions in regard to your heritage:

- What are some significant elements of your background and growing up years?
- What memories especially warm your heart?
- What positive contributions has your heritage made in your life? How has it shaped you?
- Are there things you'd change if you could?
- How can you contribute to your own culture or ethnicity?

OUR DESIGN CENTER

God sees our desires and he's not afraid of them. He made us the way we are, and he didn't create us only to ignore his design. Before we were born, God set up our design center in a way that would move in sync with him. And as we grow closer to him, our lives reflect more of his plan for us. This design center resides in our inner person, where he created our inmost being (Psalm 139:13). My inner person makes me tick, motivating and driving my life. This was a hard lesson for me to learn. For a long time I felt God's will meant doing and being something other than how I was made.

Now I know better. The journey to understanding myself has been long with many detours, but I realize now that how I'm wired on the inside should reflect my life on the outside. For most of my life, I saw myself as an extrovert. It wasn't until a few years ago, after taking a personality test from the book *Do What You Are* by Paul D. Tieger and Barbara Barron-Tieger, that I realized I tilted a little more toward introversion. That surprised me a little, but not too much. I had been realizing that I was more energized by spending time alone. That surprises some folks because my life revolves around spending time with people. However, ample time alone prepares me to interact with others in a Christlike manner and focus on their needs. When I don't have enough solitude, it's much harder for me to avoid self-centeredness.

Discovering my spiritual gifts also took a long time—no one even talked about gifts and passions in my early years of ministry. The very first spiritual gifts test I took suggested that I had the gift of mercy. I didn't really see it, but I tried to make it work. A few years later, another profile revealed that I had the gift of exhortation. That seemed to fit better. The next one suggested prophecy and teaching. Also right on. And most recently, a spiritual gifts inventory has shown strengths in the areas of leadership, discernment, words of wisdom and words of knowledge. All these gifts are lived out in my speaking, teaching, singing, liturgical dancing, life coaching and writing.

I've only recently discovered that writing is my overarching passion. I have kept a journal since junior high school, and although I haven't held on to all my journals through the years, I highly value the process of writing down my thoughts and feelings. It's therapy for me. I love to record all the thoughts, feelings and events of my life and examine how God works in them all. The journal reflects my journey with him. Periodically, I write poetry to express deep-seated feelings. I also enjoy collecting Scriptures and writing devotional thoughts to soothe my soul.

The older I get, the more fun I'm having discovering who I am. A friend of mine in her forties said recently that she was in the prime of her life. Her comment got my attention, and I thought about it for a while. Much to my surprise, I found I could say the same thing. My forties have been the best years of my adult life. At age forty-nine I'm comfortable in my own skin. I don't have to prove myself to anyone anymore.

I desire to grow continually as a person and as a woman who loves God. I'm not interested in trying to be someone else. I'm not ripped apart at the seams when someone decides they no longer want my friendship. I try to understand why so I can grow from it, but otherwise I don't try to make anyone stick around. It's been a long, hard journey getting to this place, but it's been worth the trip.

I encourage you to take time to explore your own inner design:

- How has God made you?
- What makes you tick?
- What are your passions?
- What are your spiritual gifts?
- What one thing would you like to accomplish in your life?

Getting in touch with our design center requires time and a willingness to see ourselves as God sees us. Regularly examining our lives from his perspective helps us live according to his plan. Take a quiet moment to ask God to give you his point of view. Acknowledge that you need his vision to make sense of day-to-day living, to see the events of your life not as fragmented bits but as part of a beautiful whole.

Part of our design center programming involves good works. We were created in Christ Jesus for good works, which God custom created for us before we even came into existence (Ephesians 2:10). In designing us, he wove together each delicate part so that we would play out our intended roles. For example, he knew who would have the gift of art. And in the realm of art, he knew who would sing, who would paint, who would draw, who would dance. He envisioned it long before we showed up. And he draws us to himself, saying, "Follow me, and I will show you how to live." He implores us not to miss a beat.

The Lord is eager for us to know who we are so we can walk victoriously in our purpose. Study the truths in this chapter and personalize them. I'm thankful God has never given up on me as I've tried to understand myself from his perspective. He has accompanied me every step of the way. There were many times I felt I was on the couch and Jesus was in the room counseling me. I'm grateful for God's word and prayer. They are the main resources the Holy Spirit uses to keep me connected with the Father, myself and with others.

Praise God for his good work on our behalf. The longer I walk with God, the clearer my path becomes. I'm living life based on who I am—the real me, not a pretend, people-pleasing me. I encourage you to evaluate your life by taking the following steps:

- Ask yourself, Do I know who I am in Christ? How does my life reflect my knowledge of myself in him? Am I doing what I love to do?

- Ask someone you trust to help you evaluate. Ask her what she thinks about your life at this time as a single Christian woman. Ask her if she thinks you're holding or giving your life all you can.

- Form a group to encourage and hold one another accountable to work toward realizing your dreams and passions.

- Set aside retreat hours or days for reflection and prayerful meditation.

- Slow down your pace. Guard against busyness for the sake of busyness, which will drain your spiritual passion.

As single Christian women, we have a lot to offer. As we wait for God to fulfill deep-seated desires and longings, I pray we won't just waste away. I hope we will continually pursue God and his purposes for creating us. I hope that day by day, moment by moment, we will embrace our wonderful design of transformation into the image of Christ. It is God's ultimate goal for us to look more and more like his Son. And in doing so, the world will never be the same because we will make our God-given marks on it.

QUESTIONS FOR REFLECTION OR DISCUSSION

1. How would you answer the question, Who am I?

2. Which aspects of a Christian's identity do you most relate to in this chapter?

3. In what ways do you keep yourself in the love of God, knowing and experiencing it?

4. What are your thoughts and feelings about your race as a part of your identity?

5. Define how you believe God designed you.

6. How is the Holy Spirit helping you live out your God-given design?

7. What are some good works you believe God has given you to do?

8. Do you believe you have something to offer the kingdom of God? Why or why not?

Single, Sexual and Christian—
When It Ain't All That

W hile in a Christian bookstore one day, the book *Addicted to Love* by Stephen Arterburn grabbed my eye. After looking through it, I bought it. One day, while sitting at home reading the chapter "Hooked on Sex," a reality hit me: I had been a sex addict. I was stunned, yet somewhat relieved. Mr. Arterburn's description made sense. He was talking about me.

I began reading magazines and books on sexual encounters in junior high school. I don't remember exactly how it started, but I think someone gave me the first two books. After reading those, I discovered magazines at the grocery store that I could buy, read and hide from my parents. Before I knew it, I was addicted to pornography. And for years, I wasn't convinced that pornography was wrong. Unfortunately, this habit led to a tremendous struggle with sexual lust that would affect me the rest of my life.

Pop culture feeds us a never-ending story line about how sex is the ultimate happy ending, but let me tell you—sex ain't all that when you're struggling at the very core of who you are. It ain't all that when part of you is out of control. Your story may be different from mine. You may be dealing with sexual wounds from past abuse, or you may have a history of sexual intimacy and a temptation to engage in sexual acts. Or you may simply struggle with a strong desire to have your sexual needs fulfilled. But like me, you've probably discovered one thing: Sex ain't all that!

Many years ago, when I turned down that dark sexual path, I had no idea that I would be stumbling along it for decades. I wish I could go back and undo the damage, but I can't. It's now part of my story— and I hope by telling it, I will encourage you in your own journey and let you know that there is hope for deliverance.

IN THE PIT

My sexual addiction took the form of masturbation, a habit that is often the result of loneliness, anxiety or depression. Masturbation has been described as "solo" sex, or love turned on itself. I believe masturbation is normal in the sense that many people have probably performed it at some point in their life. However, it can become a dangerous addiction. Although the Bible does not comment directly on whether masturbation is right or wrong, it does make clear that sex is to be shared between a husband and wife. Therefore, God must have a plan to help Christian single adults honor him as sexual beings—one that doesn't involve self-gratification.

When it finally dawned on me that masturbation was wrong, I tried to discuss it with a mature Christian friend, but she acted like she didn't know what I was talking about. How discouraging. I needed to share my burden with someone who could help me, but I kept it to myself awhile longer. I continued to battle with sexual thoughts and lust, and sometimes the battle raged out of control. Clearly Satan was using masturbation to enslave me and work evil in my life.

MY JOURNEY TO SEXUAL SANITY AND FREEDOM

Pornography and masturbation wreaked havoc with my life, but God showed himself strong and helped me win the fight. The battle was fierce and I wondered sometimes if I would ever be free. But through it all, I felt God's patience and concern as I cried out to him for help. Praise God, I never felt out of his grip or sphere of love. He sustained me as he began to work freedom into my life. I continued to run hard after God, reading his Word and renewing my mind. The longer I walked with him, the more I opened my heart to him. I grew to trust him more and more deeply. He understood and didn't reject me. He loved me just as I was, in all my struggles.

First, I acknowledged pornography and masturbation as sin. As hard as it was, I trained myself to stay away from sexually graphic books, magazines, songs and movies. With his strength, I stopped looking at pornography, but true freedom was a long time coming. I struggled and struggled and struggled to control my thoughts, but the pornographic images had ravaged my mind. Having a vivid, active imagination didn't help. At times I thought I would go crazy because of the inner turmoil.

Because pornography affected my mind, my physical body was also affected. The sexual urges were strong, and I knew only one way to deal with them—through masturbation. I would become fearful and out of control. I wanted to think pure thoughts. I tried quoting Scripture and rebuking the devil, often to no avail, but I didn't give up.

I kept feeding my mind with Scripture and rebuking the devil, and slowly, almost imperceptibly at first, changes began to take place. I couldn't explain it, but I knew something was different. I gradually surrendered my whole person to God—including my sexuality. I learned to be honest with him about my thoughts, feelings and urges. As I gained the courage to face the sexual part of myself head-on, I became less fearful and was able to choose not to succumb to habit. Yes, things were starting to change, and I knew it.

When sexual bondage led to feelings of shame about my body, I found help in God's Word. I didn't want to look at myself in the mirror between my neck and my knees, and most of the time I didn't. In my mind, that part of my body didn't exist, didn't belong to me. The sexual part of my body was controlled not by my spiritual nature but by the fleshly, natural and carnal part of my nature. I fully identified with Paul when he says, "I am not practicing what I would like to do, but I am doing the very thing I hate" (Romans 7:15), and also, "On the one hand I myself with my mind am serving the law of God, but on the other, with my flesh the law of sin" (Romans 7:25). He felt the war raging within. Through Christ I was able to acknowledge the shame of my body. He helped me learn to accept my body as part of his design of me.

My thought life was freed up next. I knew some sexual thoughts were normal; the key was what I did with them once they entered my mind. There were times when sex was the farthest thing from my mind, and then, boom! A sexual thought would hit me. *Where did that come from?* I wondered. I would acknowledge the thought for what it was and release it from my mind. I told it that I wasn't interested and sent it packing. Finally, sweet freedom.

It still amazes me that when I was at the lowest point of my struggle with bondage to sexual sin, God broke through. I allowed him to replace my fear with his freedom. He held me and loved me while I wrestled to become free. When I wanted to run for dear life so I wouldn't have to face the trauma and drama of my sexuality, he spoke gently to me and promised the strength to make it through. What a passage! Because Jesus died on the cross for my freedom, he made a way for me to pass through the fire.

The biggest factor in my reaching sexual sanity and freedom was the Word of God, and I still rely on it to keep me free. I immerse my mind in Scripture. I mostly read nonfiction literature that feeds my mind with truth. I'm also careful with what enters my mind. I guard my mind against sex scenes in movies or on television. I strive to keep my mind girded for action. And praise God, he is with me every step of the way.

FINDING HEALING AND DELIVERANCE

I can identify a number of critical (and sometimes tedious) stages of my journey to sexual sanity and freedom, which I think are universal to recovery from sexual addiction or temptation. If you are struggling with sexual sin, these steps can help you become free:

Have a genuine desire to change. Because sexual sin is such a stronghold, the desire for freedom is often buried beneath the layers of sin. But all change starts with desire. Without the convicting work of the Holy Spirit, change is impossible (John 16:8). And because the Holy Spirit is the Spirit of truth, he sheds the light of truth into our dark places and starts change at the root of our problem.

Confess your sexual sin to the Lord. Once the Holy Spirit has illuminated our darkness, we choose whether we will acknowledge the sin he has brought to our awareness. When we admit to the sin, 1 John 1:9 reminds us that if we confess our sin, he is faithful and just to forgive us our sin and cleanse us from all unrighteousness. In confessing sin, we agree with God on his perspective of our behavior.

Repent of your sexual sin. Once you've acknowledged your sin, repent of it. This means turning away from your sin. Turn your back on it and all it represents, and keep moving forward. Second Corinthians 7:8-11 explains the process of repentance (see also 1 Corinthians 10:13-14; 2 Timothy 2:19-22).

Rely on God's strength to help you walk in victory. Meditate and absorb Ephesians 6:10-18, which talks about the armor of God. It works!

Seek appropriate counsel. Solicit prayer support and accountability from someone godly and trustworthy. The right confidant can pray with you and help you discern whether you need professional counseling. Sexual sin can produce such a web of entanglement physically, emotionally, mentally and spiritually that a trained counselor may be necessary to help untangle the snarl. A support group or twelve-step group could also help.

Journal your thoughts. Journaling provides an outlet for your inner thoughts and feelings. The tricky part is keeping it safe from anyone who could potentially find and read it. Assess your ability to keep the journal in a safe place. The more secure it is, the more free you will feel to write the truth. Remember also that when you die, your journal will be left behind! Plan what you want done with your journals after you're gone. In my will I have named the person I want to handle my journals after I die.

Immerse yourself in God's Word. In case you hadn't noticed, this is one of my top suggestions for any situation. God's Word has the power to affect our heart like no one and nothing else; we have to decide whether we will allow it to do its supernatural work (Hebrews 4:12).

Learn how to be alone. Avoid the need to be with someone else when doing so could lead to sexual sin. When we learn who we are in Christ, we experience fullness of life. We see him for who he is, and his Spirit sheds light on who we are. Get to know yourself. Stop wanting to be someone else at the expense of knowing yourself. Take time to reflect on what's really in your heart—explore hobbies, talents and gifts. Trust God to bring the right people into your life in his time.

HOLDING ON
TO JESUS

As I think about what freedom from sexual sin looks like, I'm reminded of Isaiah 43:18-19: "Do not call to mind the former things, or ponder things of the past. Behold, I will do something new, now it will spring forth; will you not be aware of it? I will even make a roadway in the wilderness, rivers in the desert." That is exactly what God did for me and will do for you.

SEXUAL WOUNDS

According to Dr. Mark Laaser in *Talking to Your Kids About Sex*, a third of all women and a fourth of all men have experienced some form of sexual abuse. Sexual trauma includes things like molestation, rape and incest. The pain of this kind of abuse runs deep and the journey is long when you're seeking answers, healing and wholeness.

Arlene, who told me that her name means "a pawn or something that is used," has felt exactly like that—something used—most of her life. Arlene was molested by her father from age seven to eleven. As if that weren't enough for one person to carry, she was raped at age eighteen.

Arlene remembers feeling shame as a little girl. As she grew older she became angry with her mother. She wondered, "Where were you when I needed you?" After she was raped she began asking herself, "Is there something defective in me? Am I sending out signals? Am I crazy? Is this the way the world operates?" Questions flooded her mind and soul.

As a result of her traumatic past, Arlene dealt with fear, shame, secrecy, lack of trust, a sense of powerlessness and control issues. She knew that as a child of God she was loved by him, but she needed to know that he wouldn't forget her in her pain. And although she knew God loved her, she was afraid that if others knew her, they wouldn't.

So she lived a life of secrecy. "How can you not feel shame when you're told to keep a secret like this?" she asks. "In my mind I was trying to make the abuse OK. But it wasn't OK. Sexual abuse takes a toll on confidence and self-worth. I felt like a Raggedy Ann doll that had been tossed aside with its eyes pulled out."

Arlene still struggles with knowing who to trust and how to set healthy boundaries. This sometimes carried over to her spiritual connection with God. She used to wonder if God could be trusted and whether he really loved her. This doubt led to a sense of powerlessness and weakness. Power can produce change, she says, but without it, change is hard to come by.

Through years of hard work and prayer, Arlene is finally learning to cope with her past and be at peace. "I feel the need to control some area of my life, a safe place, which helps my sense of powerlessness," she says. "My home has been that one safe place. However, in recognizing the truth, I've come to realize that Christ is the only safe, trustworthy place. It's taken me a long time to get there."

Healing of sexual wounds is a long, slow process. No one knows this better than Arlene, who offers this insight from her journey: "Don't cover up abuse. Don't keep it a secret. The truth makes you free. Find someone trustworthy and tell your story. See the part you played in covering it up. Hopefully there will come a time when you're no longer willing to live a lie but would rather be free in Jesus. We try to make our world work for us on our own, but healing can't occur if we're not willing to face the truth."

THE SEARCH FOR INTIMACY

Everyone desires love, acceptance and intimacy. We want to be vulnerable without being slam-dunked. But sometimes we mistakenly equate intimacy with sex, and when we confuse the two, we discover once again that sex ain't all that. Instead of being a good gift from God, it becomes a poison.

From my discussions with women, it appears that the desire for love, affection and commitment is the primary motivation for sexual activity. For men, however, sexual intercourse is often an end in itself. My friend Kris shared with me about her search for intimacy and hopes that other women will make better choices than she did. Here's her story:

> I'm from an upper middle class family. I always did very well in school—I graduated from college and had a very successful ca-

reer. But when it came to love, I was stupid. I didn't have a clue what true love was really about. I used to connect love with sex, which meant I always had to have a guy in my life. Sex made me feel loved. I was jealous of other girls who had boyfriends when I didn't, thinking they were loved and I wasn't. This mindset led to many stupid mistakes. Though I didn't want to disappoint my parents and was afraid of diseases and pregnancy, I was more afraid of not being loved.

Over the years I had sex with several guys, a few times without protection. Luckily I didn't get any diseases. But I did get pregnant—twice. The first time, I broke up with my boyfriend and a month later, with the support of family and "friends," had an abortion. A week after that my boyfriend was arrested for trying to break down the door of my house. The police found a knife in his pocket. That boyfriend stalked me for two years, and I had to take him to court for threatening me. Was that love?

You would think after that mess that I would have found joy in being unattached. And I did stay single and dateless for about five years while my career took off. During that time I concentrated on promotions and raises. My success fulfilled me—at least I thought it did. There was a part of me that longed to be loved, but I still didn't know anything about true love or joy. So I started dating a guy, and even though I didn't love him I had sex with him, lived with him and made a baby with him. We decided we'd better get married, though I knew he wasn't the one for me.

Kris did get married and had a beautiful daughter. But her marriage hit many bumps, and she and her husband have been separated for years now. Intermittent attempts at reconciliation have never developed into permanent recommitment. They remain separated, and Kris continues her quest to develop greater intimacy with the Lord, the one who knows and loves her best.

As you well know, Kris is not the only woman who has given her body outside of marriage because of a deep longing for intimacy—not by far. The need for closeness and vulnerability has led many women (and men) to make choices they wouldn't otherwise. But what are we supposed to do with those needs if we're not married? They certainly don't just go away. Fortunately, there are ways we can experience intimacy in a healthy way within God's will. As a single adult, I need friends who love me unconditionally. I'm grateful for the few friends in my life who allow me the freedom to fail. These friends are safe. Communication is open and honest. We each want to become the kind of intimate friend the other needs.

A safe relationship with an eligible man who does not demand sex may also lead to genuine closeness. If we prevent physical involvement from undermining a caring relationship, we can reach a healthy level of nonsexual affection that may even lead to a permanent commitment in marriage—though obviously not always.

HOLDING ON TO JESUS

In the midst of the sexual revolution of our day, how do we as single Christian adults honor and love God with our bodies? By loving him with all our hearts. In developing a love relationship with him, we come to know that he loves us and we love him back through a life of gratitude, worship and obedience. As we grow in love for God, we develop the capacity to love our bodies. We become a "vessel for honor, sanctified, useful to the Master, prepared for every good work" (2 Timothy 2:21). Hallelujah!

OVERCOMING SEXUAL SIN

Left unchecked, sexual sin leads to sexual entanglement, which leads to sexual bondage. Sexual bondage is like a web; no matter which way you turn, there seems to be no way out. Again, the apostle Paul sums it up: "It happens so regularly that it's predictable. The moment I decide to do good, sin is there to trip me up. I truly delight in God's commands, but it's pretty obvious that not all of me joins in that delight. Parts of me covertly rebel, and just when I least expect it, they take charge. I've tried everything and nothing helps. I'm at the end of my rope. Is there no one who can do anything for me? Isn't that the real question?" (Romans 7:21-24 *The Message*).

Scripture also tells us that Christ bought our freedom (Galatians 5:1); therefore we can shake off sin. A friend shares how God transformed her life and gave her freedom in this area:

> Being a single Christian is summed up in the word *surrender*—to his way of seeing and doing things. In surrender I'm experiencing a whole different paradigm, a frame of reference that I have not known nor would have chosen for myself.
>
> When I finally surrendered to God, my views about sexuality went out the window in light of his way and Word. There's no real way to deal with our sexuality outside of his design and will. We tend to come away from the world with the idea that sex is something we must have even if we're not in a permanent relationship with someone. We think we can't be healthy without that level of companionship and physical interaction.
>
> Now I know that I don't *have* to have premarital sex. In surrender to him, God grows up our definition of love and who we are. Over time, the sexual thing becomes very small. We can focus on it and make it something big, or realize that sex outside of marriage has nothing to do with love. When we're honest, we admit that having premarital sex is a way of getting intimacy on the sly, without really committing. We want to enjoy the sex without the commitment of marriage.

I'm thankful the Lord let me live long enough to see why he makes the commandments he makes. We're blessed to learn from the right side of the fence rather than the wrong side. He loved me through my sin and eventually my heart just broke down. I said, "Lord, I can finally see your love for me."

ULTIMATE INTIMACY

Intimacy with God is the ultimate joy we can aspire to. Only he knows us inside and out, in the most intricate detail, because he created us. Giving God his rightful place and proper ownership in our lives gives us meaning, purpose and a sense of belonging. As we learn to develop intimacy with God first, he brings healing and wholeness to our sexuality. As we walk closely with him, we can enjoy our sexuality to his honor and glory.

QUESTIONS FOR REFLECTION OR DISCUSSION

1. What Scriptures have shaped your beliefs about human sexuality?
2. What are your thoughts on pornography and masturbation?
3. What areas of sexual purity do you struggle with? How can you experience freedom in these areas?
4. What is your reaction to the author's journey to sexual sanity and freedom?
5. Review the steps of freedom from sexual sin. Have you ever needed to take steps like these? Explain.
6. Have you experienced sexual wounds? How have you dealt with them?

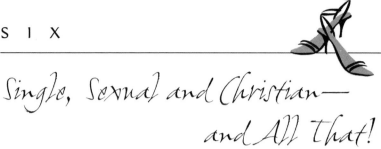

Single, Sexual and Christian— and All That!

So what do I do with the fact that I am a single, sexual Christian woman? The Bible makes it clear that God designed sex for procreation and enjoyment. Yet I'm taught to remain pure. I'm not married; therefore the sexual part of me can't be fulfilled that way. So, I ask again, what do I do with my sexuality—something theologians keep telling me is a blessing from God? Have you ever asked these questions? I have. Many times.

A THEOLOGY OF SEXUALITY

Human sexuality was God's idea, a part of his original plan. According to Genesis 1:26-27, "God said, 'Let us make humankind in our image, according to our likeness.' . . . So God created humankind in his image, / in the image of God He created them; / male and female he created them" (NRSV). Genesis 5:1-2 says, "This is the list of the descendants of Adam. When God created humankind, he made them in the likeness of God. Male and female he created them, and he blessed them and named them 'Humankind' when they were created" (NRSV). In Genesis 9:6 we read, "In his own image / God made humankind" (NRSV). God's conclusion: "God saw everything that he had made, and indeed, it was very good" (Genesis 1:31 NRSV).

As image bearers of God, our sexuality reflects who we are, not merely what we do. In the Old Testament, the law and the Spirit's visitation showed the way for the image bearers to live. In the New Testament, the new covenant through Jesus and the Holy Spirit show us the way. As part of God's representation on earth, he created women in his image and likeness.

Living as authentic, single and sexual women, we seek to live according to God's plan and purpose. We realize that although we have reproductive organs that determine our sex, we're more than our reproductive organs. Unfortunately, because of poor teaching and misogynistic attitudes, many Christian girls and women still feel deep down that men are closer to the image of God, more like Christ than females can ever be. This is a lie.

Although we are each created to be unique, if you think about the women you know, you will notice a pattern of wonderful characteristics that reflect the character of God. For example, many of us are able to listen well. We're perceptive and sensitive to the needs of others. We're multitaskers. We're both gentle and strong. We're caregivers. We enjoy encouraging others. We're influencers. We're verbal. We're equipped with a great capacity to love and be loved. We're nesters, creating a home environment and a place of solace and rest.

God's character and ways are exhibited in us through Christ, so that all of our feminine characteristics reflect him. According to 2 Corinthians 3:18, as we see the Lord's glory, we're transformed into the image of his glory. We have the treasure of the gospel of Jesus Christ in us. Because of this, we have God's power dwelling within to show forth his glory in who we are and what we do. So, single, sexual Christian women, we have the power to use our bodies to the glory of God. Amen! And how do we do that?

We bring glory to God by remembering that our bodies belong to him. First Corinthians 6 reminds us what's what: our body is for the Lord and the Lord is for our body. The passage assumes we know that our bodies are members of Christ. Our body is also a temple of the Holy Spirit who is in us, who was given to us by God. Our bodies were bought with a price; therefore we're to glorify God in and through them (1 Corinthians 6:18-20).

Romans 12:1-2 admonishes us to present our bodies as living and holy sacrifices, acceptable to God, which is our spiritual service of worship. The passage gives us a clue about how we carry this out. We avoid conforming to the world's ideas and standards by renewing our minds according to God's Word. As our minds are renewed, we're transformed, showing forth God's good, acceptable and perfect will. We aren't to think that we have it so together that we cannot fall, but to think reasonably with the amount of faith given to us. Based on Philippians 1:20, we can adopt Paul's desire that our bodies won't be put to shame in anything.

EARLY INFLUENCES

What do you think about your sexuality? How did you learn about sexuality? What experiences have contributed to your present perspective? Who has influenced your views? We need to be aware of how our own story affects us and the way we think. Explore the following questions as you think of your sexuality:

- Did your parents teach you about sexuality when you were growing up? How? Remember that there are nonverbal ways of teaching. The way your parents related to each other, for example, taught you a lot about sexuality—for good or ill. So did the way they dressed and carried themselves, the way they responded when your body started changing in puberty, and their silence. If they never said anything about sexuality, they may have communicated to you that it's dangerous and indecent.

- Was sex education taught in your school? How was it taught and what did you learn?

- What kind of training on sexuality did you receive in your church or other religious institution, if any?
- What did you learn from your friends about sexuality?
- Are there current sexual issues you need to resolve in your life? Do you know where you can find help?

What is your perspective today compared with the way you grew up? Who or what influences your sexuality now? Do you feel you're in a healthy, safe place sexually? In what ways are you safeguarding and maintaining yourself in a manner pleasing to God? The sexual revolution is moving full speed ahead. We must stay alert to the sexual temptations all around us.

In a recent message on purity in a sex-saturated society, Dr. Keith Wood gave five intriguing facts:

1. Those who abstain from sexual intercourse before marriage report the highest levels of sexual satisfaction in marriage.

2. Those who cohabitate before marriage have a fifty percent higher divorce rate than those who do not.

3. Those who abstain from sexual intercourse before marriage have the highest rates of fidelity in marriage.

4. The introduction of sex in a dating relationship almost always ushers in the breakup of that relationship.

5. Sexually transmitted diseases (including AIDS) can remain dormant for up to a decade or more but be passed on to others during that time.

Fully, Healthily Sexual

What does it look like for celibate singles to be fully, healthily sexual without promiscuity, without repression and without resorting to masturbation or pornography? What does it look like? It looks like *purity*.

Paul in 1 Thessalonians 4:2-6 gives clear instructions for living a life of purity. The Lord made it plain in this Scripture to make sure we get it. It's God's will that we abstain from sexual immorality. It's God's will that we control our bodies in holiness and honor, not giving in to lustful passion like people do who don't know God. And it's God's will that we don't wrong or exploit a brother or sister in this area. God calls us to purity; it's his idea. He commands it for our good and his glory. Purity: those six letters spell something beautiful. Purity begins in the heart and affects our mind, our will, our emotions, our body and our relationships. As we walk in purity, we walk in a manner that pleases God.

Pleasing God with a pure heart. True purity starts with a personal relationship with Jesus Christ. As we grow in relationship with God, our desire to sin against him lessens. We begin losing desires we once had. Although we may struggle like Paul did in Romans 7, doing what we don't want and not doing what we want, our hearts have changed because of Christ, and we really will want what he wants.

Pleasing God with our mind and will. Philippians 4:8 used to plague me: "Whatever is true, whatever is honorable, whatever is right, whatever is pure, whatever is lovely, whatever is of good repute, if there is any excellence and if anything worthy of praise, dwell on these things." I thought to myself, "Come on, God. You really don't think I can set my mind that way, do you?" Assuredly, learning to think on these things and setting our mind on things above (Colossians 3:1) comes with practice—lots of it. Memorizing and meditating on God's Word supernaturally affects our mind as well as our will; it can turn our course of action. We start to act differently, and in so doing we promote the gospel of Jesus Christ (Ephesians 5:15-17; 1 Corinthians 9:23-27). If we're not absorbing Scripture, whatever we are putting into our minds will affect us. Even though romance novels and romantic comedies seem harmless, they can fuel the longing for sex and compromise a life of purity.

Pleasing God with our emotions. Emotions have a physiological basis. When we're healthy and strong, we're more likely to experience positive emotions. Exercising, eating right, cultivating satisfying friendships and enjoying the beauty of nature all promote a healthy emotional life. Emotions are part of our spiritual life as well. God shares our griefs and our joys. Though sometimes we can grit our teeth and ignore a bad mood, we can also choose to practice Philippians 4:8 on an emotional level as well.

Pleasing God with our body. This is probably the area in which most people struggle to please God. The power of our sex drive sometimes seems to override everything else. Sexual urges are not wrong or bad, just hard to control. Channeling the powerful, natural, God-given urges that we experience requires us to act proactively. We monitor what goes into our minds. We don't watch certain movies or TV shows because of the sexual content. We don't listen to certain songs or read certain magazines or books for the same reason. We try not to obsess over the desire to be in a relationship. Sometimes, however, even when we're proactive, we still experience sexual urges. In either case, how do we respond? Here's a plan for dealing with these situations:

- First, don't feel guilty. You were created as a sexual being.

- Second, stop and question why you are being aroused. Is it something you saw, heard, felt, thought?

- Third, remove yourself from the source of stimulation once you've identified it.

- Fourth, redirect your sexual urges through prayer. Talk to God about what you're going through. Be honest and ask for his help. He has the understanding and power to disengage the urge.

- Fifth, read your Bible. Know passages that speak of the power of God in your life. I've found that the more time I spend in Scripture, the less I experience sexual urges.

- Sixth, share your desire for control in this area with someone you trust. Ask her to hold you accountable.
- Seventh, stay on the alert and keep your mind filled with the things of the Lord.
- Eighth, exercise. It provides an outlet for built-up energy.

Pleasing God with our relationships. In this aspect of purity, we surround ourselves with people who spur us on in our faith. We continually point others to Christ and his will for their lives. As we seek to love, respect and care for others, we learn to do the same for ourselves. The power of our sexuality can be channeled toward cultivating the fruit of the Spirit in our interactions with others. And though she is not always perfect, the single, sexual Christian woman pursues God passionately and wants to know his will for her life. She is fully alive in Christ unashamedly, trusting him to make her more like himself.

Jill is a divorced single woman who has found creative ways to maintain her purity and make the most of her life. Here's what she has to say:

> Being sexually healthy is a deep dimension of being emotionally, spiritually and physically healthy. It is *not* easy to be sexually alive as a single person, but if you shut off this dimension of yourself, you forfeit the capacity for other kinds of intimacy and delight in God's world.
>
> Stay physically active; walk and run and play games outside rather than just going to the gym. Enjoy the creation—gardening, hiking and going to the beach. Smell and taste and touch things—tree bark, flowing water, soil and flowers. The earth will bless you.
>
> Love everything beautiful. Take care of your body—eat well, exercise, dress simply but with care. Honor your body as God's habitation. Ground yourself deeply in God's love for you; take time to meditate on that love and revel in it. That's the best pro-

tection against emotional neediness, which can express itself in sexual hunger. God doesn't promise to be everything for us emotionally; it wasn't good for Adam to be alone, so from the beginning people have been made for human as well as divine companionship. But no human love can meet our most profound need; only God's love does. It tells us who we are, gives us great dignity and calls us into a life of meaning.

Take your work seriously. This relates to sexuality because it's a productive way to sublimate physical and emotional need. Pour creative energy into your daily work, volunteer ministry, music, art, writing or dance. Work in a team whenever possible. You do need "vocational intimacy"—think of the apostle Paul, who always traveled and ministered with others.

Cultivate friendships; give loving attention to others; stay close to wise friends who can help you discern healthy choices. A rich "friend and family tree" of many branches will channel your energy in positive directions. Hug your friends (we're made to be touched), and be sure to find children to play with. Of course you want to steer away from inappropriate intimacy; getting too close to the wrong person is setting yourself up for

---

HOLDING ON
TO JESUS

In finding Jesus, we find who he really is, and when we embrace him not only as Savior but as our very life, we begin to "taste and see that the LORD is good" (Psalm 34:8). We begin to know that no good thing does he withhold from those who seek him (Psalm 34:10). Our eyes are opened to the truth of life—life in the realm of the will of God, the one who created us and knows us best.

heartache, if not sexual trespass. I really believe being sexually healthy is tied in with being healthy in every other area.

A GARDEN IN EXILE

As Jeremiah exhorted the Babylonian exiles, so his words exhort us as single, sexual Christian women. For many (though not all) of you single women, being unmarried makes you feel like you're in exile from the good things of the Lord. I pray Jeremiah's words will give you hope and encouragement.

Interestingly enough, God says he is the one who sent the Israelites into exile (Jeremiah 29:4). He did this because of their sins as the nation, not necessarily their individual sins. Jeremiah tells the exiles how to live to the glory of God and their own benefit. He says, "Build houses and live in them; and plant gardens and eat their produce" (Jeremiah 29:5). The key is to find ways to live to the fullest, allowing God to give you the good in your life.

As I mentioned earlier, women are natural nesters. We like our home environment to feel warm and safe, to look pretty. A great way to put Jeremiah's words into practice in your own life is to evaluate your home and think of ways to make it warm and restful for you. Flowers, plants, the right colors and Scripture verses can all add a sense of life to your environment. An awareness of Christ's presence helps warm up an atmosphere of loneliness, so cultivate this awareness by playing Christian music, reading Scripture and lining the walls with prayer. Invite Christian friends over who build and uplift you. Remind yourself what you're thankful for; an attitude of gratitude helps keep your home cheery.

Jeremiah continues, "Seek the welfare of the city where I have sent you into exile, and pray to the LORD on its behalf, for in its welfare you will find your welfare" (Jeremiah 29:7). We can make a huge difference in the community where we live. We can get involved in a local church. We can seek out volunteer opportunities in our neighborhoods. Think of ways God can use you to impact the world for his kingdom right outside your front door. Pray for your community's welfare and safety.

I have seen the effectiveness of praying for a community firsthand. At one point, the neighborhood where I grew up and where my elderly mother lived started to decline. Drugs and violence moved in. Because mom lived there and I frequently visited her, we were acutely aware of what was happening. I admit that mostly out of concern for my mom's safety I joined her in praying for the neighborhood. As we faithfully prayed, God answered in big ways. We saw troublemakers carted off and stopped, and the crime subsided. Mom and I were grateful to see God's hand at work.

And then there's the well-known verse, Jeremiah 29:11, which says, "For surely I know the plans I have for you, says the LORD, plans for your welfare and not for harm, to give you a future with hope" (NRSV). Sometimes when God doesn't give us what we want, we question whether his plans are for good and not harm. We wonder why God doesn't move when he sees our hearts hurting. Like Job when he questioned God, we also want to know why God allows things to happen the way they do. Praise God that he didn't leave Job hanging. He responded in a mighty way in chapters 40—42. Ponder those chapters and see if God may not be asking you some of the same questions as you wait on him to fulfill his perfect will for you moment by moment, day by day.

Finally, Jeremiah 29:12-14 says, "'Then when you call upon me and come and pray to me, I will hear you. When you search for me, you will find me; if you seek me with all your heart, I will let you find me,' says the LORD, 'and I will restore your fortunes and gather you from all the nations and all the places where I have driven you,' says the LORD, 'and I will bring you back to the place from which I sent you into exile'" (NRSV). God is not afraid of our prayers or our honesty. He welcomes the truth from our innermost being. He promises to answer our prayers according to what is best for us.

My heart has been comforted many times throughout the years by 1 John 5:14-15, which states, "This is the confidence which we have before Him, that, if we ask anything according to His will, He hears us. And if we know that He hears us in whatever we ask, we know that we have the requests which we have asked from Him." We can trust him.

QUESTIONS FOR REFLECTION OR DISCUSSION

1. How would you describe or define "being female"?

2. Do you see yourself as conforming to the cultural norms of femininity, or do you depart from them in some ways?

3. Beginning with the Scripture verses cited in this chapter, devise your own theology of sexuality, and think about how you would express that.

4. What do you think about the creative suggestions Jill gave in making the most of her single life?

5. How does the Jeremiah 29 passage make you feel?

6. How is God calling you to make a garden within what sometimes feels like the "exile" of singleness?

7. How can you please God with your heart, mind, will, body and relationships?

8. Can you think of other ways, along with the ones listed, to redirect your sexual urges? Or do you even want to? Explain.

Intimacy with Others

I've enjoyed getting to know Leslee, a new friend, and sharing in her zeal for God. One day I asked her to share her thoughts on intimacy with others. She readily accepted my request. This is what she shared:

> Most people who confuse intimacy with sex find themselves disappointed after the climatic end (if they're lucky to get to that point). Then they realize that sex is not what they were looking for at all.
>
> Intimacy is the art of knowing someone so well you almost feel they're a part of you. You know their thoughts ahead of time. You share your true self with them because you know it's safe to do so. You're not ridiculed, mocked or scorned. You're simply allowed to be who you are. Intimacy can occur between couples, same-sex friends and family members. So why do we look for it only in sexual partners?
>
> I have spent my life looking for intimacy. I have been blessed to find it with my two girlfriends, but I have yet to find it with a mate or potential mate. While married for ten years, I tried to develop it with my husband, but I was too wounded and emotionally immature. Now that I'm divorced, I think there were times when my husband and I were intimate, but there were too

many other things lacking in the relationship for true intimacy to survive.

Now as a divorced forty-year-old entering the dating realm for the first time (I never dated anyone other than my ex-husband), I find it difficult to allow myself to be intimate on that level. Sexual, yes. Intimate, no. I'm afraid of allowing myself to be vulnerable and potentially hurt again. I don't want to waste that inner part of myself on just anyone. I don't want to open up to anyone who's only interested in sex.

Unfortunately, I've found that more men are interested in sex than in cultivating intimacy. Could they also be afraid and overly cautious? Sure! But sex for me has never filled the void. I've tried everything from one-night stands to sexual relationships that lasted for several months. There was never any sharing of our true selves, just physical contact. So I search on for true intimacy.

I have experienced my own frustration in seeking intimacy with others. While in Bible college I met Robert. He was kind and he was a gentleman. He was solid in his faith and in the Word of God. His physical appearance was attractive, and so was his walk with God. I enjoyed his warm smile, big eyes and the small dosages of attention he gave me. I found myself wondering if he was just kind or if he was interested in a relationship. His kind acts continued over a period of several weeks. Rather than string myself along, I prayed about talking with him. I figured we were both mature Christians, so we should be able to talk about our feelings as adults. So I got up the courage one day to ask him if he was interested in something more than friendship. He responded that he was extending kindness toward me and that was all. I thanked him for his honesty. Although I was disappointed, I respected him and myself for clearing the air. We continued to be kind to one another as we carried on with our lives.

Relating to and seeking intimacy with others can be challenging and sometimes frustrating. These words from my journal catch a wave of my frustration: "Father, help me in developing intimacy with others when I don't feel like it. Sometimes it seems easier to go it alone. Why can't it just be you and me? And yet I know the answer to that question. You created me for community no matter how hard it is sometimes. Thank you for your design."

I'm thankful for God's patience with me as I learn and grow in relating with others. I'm also thankful for the patience of the people closest to me, for their availability and friendship.

What Is It that We Want?

So what is intimacy anyway? I've heard it described as "into me see," inviting someone else to get to know us for who we really are. This description seems fair. The invitation involves a willingness to be vulnerable, to let the real thing hang out! It means believing that someone is safe enough to be trusted with our innermost thoughts and feelings. Angela, a friend of mine, feels this way:

> The word *intimacy* evokes many different emotions. Being a divorced woman, my immediate thought goes to physical intimacy. While a man no longer fills that need, I do have a wonderful eleven-year-old daughter that has filled the basic needs of closeness with hugs and kisses on a daily basis for the past eight years of being single again.
>
> Emotional intimacy is found through my personal relationship with Jesus Christ. I have found that walking and talking with the Lord daily is the most crucial way to meet my needs for intimacy. Also, the Lord has surrounded me with wonderful family and friends over the years who have met my needs in a physical sense. A lot of trial and error goes into determining who to trust. Nevertheless, through the process, I've learned to

pray for discernment and ask God to bring the people into my life who can fill those areas of need for me and vice versa.

I've only recently come to learn the value of having godly Christian male friends. Female friends have been my backbone and the ones I can count on. But there is value in having a man as a friend. A man's perspective is much different than a woman's on any given topic, and I've found it invaluable to have both in my life.

We all long for intimacy with God and others. Often because we've been hurt, we retreat from intimacy, afraid to trust one more time. If we're not careful we can build walls, depriving ourselves of the rewards and satisfaction of true intimacy. I asked several women to tell me what prevented them from experiencing intimacy. They mentioned

- disloyalty
- lying
- feeling misunderstood
- feeling unappreciated
- sarcasm
- not feeling heard
- anger
- fear (of rejection, of exposure or getting hurt)
- sin
- busyness
- past hurts
- pride
- laziness or lack of effort
- not being deliberate or intentional
- not knowing how

- self-absorption
- lack of a role model
- lack of self-awareness (in not knowing who you are, it's hard to share yourself with someone else)

As we strive to counteract such intimacy breakers, we position ourselves to receive and give intimacy in our relationships. And we can count on the fact that God's love is unchanging. We can rest in the stability of his unchanging love and trust him to help us communicate his love to others. We need his gentle lovingkindness.

UNSAFE PEOPLE

Throughout our lives we encounter all kinds of people—the kindred spirit who builds us up, the bully who tears us down and the emotional vampire who sucks us dry. We have to decide what we will do with each relationship. Sometimes, before we know it, we're vulner-

---

HOLDING ON TO JESUS

As you think about your life and ponder the following Scriptures, ask God to speak to you. Could there be truth here he's been trying to show you for a long time?

"Your goodness is so great! You have stored up great blessings for those who honor you. You have done so much for those who come to you for protection, blessing them before the watching world." (Psalm 31:19 NLT)

"If you then, being evil, know how to give good gifts to your children, how much more will your Father who is in heaven give what is good to those who ask Him!" (Matthew 7:11 NASB)

able with a person who doesn't mean us good or who has no concept of healthy boundaries. It takes time to learn discernment of character so we can spot these kinds of people.

Drs. Henry Cloud and John Townsend, in their book *Safe People,* describe the kind of individuals we should be wary of. Unsafe people quite often appear winsome and promising but have hidden character problems. They avoid closeness instead of connecting—or they try to force intimacy prematurely or inappropriately. They are more concerned about "I" than "we." They avoid freedom instead of encouraging it. They flatter us instead of confronting us. Unsafe people condemn us instead of forgiving us. They stay in parent-child roles instead of relating as equals. Unsafe people are unstable over time instead of being consistent. They have a negative influence on us. Unsafe people gossip instead of keeping secrets.

You probably have at least one person who comes to mind as you reflect on these traits—an unsafe person whose life has intersected with yours at some point. Unsafe people leave a trail of tears behind them and have a path of wounding ahead of them. Sometimes the need to feel loved is so great that we attach ourselves to anyone, without first determining whether the relationship is a good idea. We need to stay alert and honest in our interactions—not paranoid, just watchful and wise. The first line of defense in protecting ourselves is allowing ourselves to be loved by God first. Second, we can deliberately seek out safe people to invest our lives in and allow them to invest in us. Thank God for safe people. They give us hope as we continuously face the unsafe people in our lives.

Safe people make us better people by their very presence. They help us become the person God intended us to be by spurring us on to bear good fruit. The safe person does keep some boundaries—she's warm and kind, but she doesn't share every secret and shed all reserve with just anybody. She gets her primary nurturing from God so she isn't desperate for friendship. This healthy restraint may make a needy person feel anxious or angry, but the safe person wants a reciprocal relationship within appropriate limits.

Safe people prove trustworthy over time. They are not defensive when confronted and own it when they are wrong. They take responsibility for their lives. They admit their weaknesses and are humble. Safe people consistently express care and concern for others' well-being, but they also know how to care for themselves. Safe people are relationship-centered and empathetic. In case you haven't already guessed, a safe person is not only someone we want in our lives, but someone we want to be!

Close relationships work for or against personal growth. When evaluating someone's character, look at these traits in terms of degree. For example, we all lie at some time in some way, but chronic liars are dangerous. Growing Christians desire to change. If you're in a relationship and notice some unhealthy patterns, confront your friend gently. If they seem willing to change, forgive them and work with them. You'll be a safe person contributing to their growth. But if they resist, proceed with caution, or even walk away.

Consider the following suggestions:

- Acknowledge to yourself the unhealthiness of the relationship.
- Hold on to the reality that the relationship is unhealthy.
- Pray, pray, pray for God's wisdom and strength to inaugurate change or to walk away.
- Express clearly to the other person your perception of why the relationship is unhealthy and why you need to dissolve it if changes are not made.
- Decide on time apart while working on changes. Come together no more than twice a month with no more than weekly phone calls.
- Have an objective, trusted person hold you accountable. Report

back to them after each encounter with your difficult person.

- Over a period of six months, assess growth and development of the relationship or lack thereof.
- If there are no signs of change, walk away by God's grace and strength.
- By all means, if you determine that your life is in physical danger, get help and run fast!

Sometimes calling a halt to a relationship can wake a person up enough to cause her to reevaluate her behavior and possibly execute change. Then later you can resume the relationship in a healthier way.

I asked my friend Marsha how she has developed deep friendships. She responded, "Through a lot of hard work in communicating with friends over the years, and by building trusting relationships in promises kept. I've sought a variety of friends with different interests and have learned from them. And by being vulnerable with them, I've allowed them to minister to me."

In the book *Friendship that Runs Deep*, Keith Anderson calls mutual encouragement "the glue for healthy relationships." Encouragement sticks us together and refuels our empty tanks with fresh courage. We all need someone who is a voice of encouragement in our lives, because other people drain our tanks through insincere flattery, constant criticism or desperate need. In addition to affirmation, we also need the encouragement of truth spoken in love. There are two people who will tell you the truth: your enemy who hates you and your friend who loves you. Your enemy tells the truth to hurt you, but your friend wants to help you grow. Can you think of at least one person who will tell you the truth even if it hurts? Real friends won't lie to each other to spare the friendship. They honor and encourage one another while understanding the value of truth. I would rather have a difficult truth spoken to me than a pleasant lie.

Do you have at least one soul friend? Someone who will ask you what God is doing in your life, what you're holding back from him, what you're celebrating, what you're grieving? Someone of whom you can ask those same questions? This kind of openness provides a sense of welcome and healthy closeness. We need people who propel us to greater godliness, people who are passionate in their relationship with God and pursuing him with all their heart.

Praise God, I can think of several friends who encourage me consistently. I love the notes, phone calls, e-mails and visits. They want to know how I'm doing. They pray for me, and I know it. I can tell. I am eternally grateful for these friends who love me, encourage me and invest prayerfully in my life.

ALL KINDS OF FAMILY

My greatest cheerleader and listener in life died five years ago. That person was my mom. Mom was actually my great-aunt. She and Dad adopted me when I was a baby and they loved and nourished me with all they had to offer. Mom lived after Dad died for almost seventeen years. Those years without Dad brought us even closer together.

God gave me another godly great-aunt, my Aunt Florrie. She loves me well, and I praise God for her. We became closer during Mom's illness and through her death. I remember the meals, the prayers and the warm hugs during that difficult time of my life. Like Mom, she spurs me on to greater faith in God and a life of holiness to his glory.

Some family relationships are strained, even destructive, and we have to learn to keep a healthy distance for our own sanity—and sometimes safety. However, for most of us, our family is an essential part of our support. If you have a loving relationship with your family, try not to take them for granted even though it's easy to do. Keep the lines of communication open. Try to see the other person's viewpoint even while sharing your own. Visit as you can. Try to allow the fruit of the Holy Spirit to flow from you to your family. Give to them in special ways as they give to you, showing that you appreciate their lovingkindness.

When biological family members aren't close by, God sometimes gives us other people who become like family. I live in the basement apartment of a home occupied by a family of six. Dave and Liz along with their kids embraced me during the illness and death of my mother. I will never forget their act of love in driving a total of four hundred miles to meet Mom before she died. They continue to bless me.

Three little blond-headed boys named Harrison, Garrett and Samuel belong to Karen and Barry Vaughan, who have allowed their sons to be an integral and special part of my life. These little boys are the closest I've come to having babies of my own to watch grow up. They call me Auntie, which gets us lots of baffled looks when we're together since I'm African American and they're as Caucasian as they come. I love it.

When my mom died I was overcome with the reality of being an orphan. Two women reached out to me after that loss, and their words were almost identical. Now that Mom was gone, they each wanted to be a mother to me and take care of me. So now I have two moms to fill the gap: Addie, an African American woman who has known me since nursing school, and Susan, a Caucasian woman from my previous church. I laughed as I told them that I now have a black mama and a white one, one who lives in the South and one in the North. I'm covered from coast to coast. God is good.

When we discover a potentially healthy friendship, we have a choice. Will we allow the friendship to grow? Or will we walk away, refusing to let ourselves be vulnerable or willing to receive? I could have resisted Addie and Susan to protect myself—and missed out on their wonderful friendship. As single adults, we need relationships with families. We need to reach out to them and they need to reach out to us. Some of us need to take our focus off praying for a husband and start praying for these kinds of people to come into our lives.

MENTORING AND SERVING OTHERS

I have a strong maternal instinct and enjoy caring for others. Mentoring and discipleship create community for me. I'm thankful for the women and men who allow me to coach them through life. The women are "my girls," and we've walked through joys and sorrows together. They've challenged me to stay faithful to God. The young men are affectionately known as my spiritual sons. They bring joy and flavor to my life, and I'm thankful for their godly influence for the kingdom of God.

Linda, the women's ministry director of a local church, has been my prayer partner for several years. We're honest with each other and encourage each other to be all God has in mind for us. We challenge and confront in love because we don't want to miss God's will for our lives. As women in ministry, we want to lead by example.

And then there are Brenda and Keith, a husband and wife with a heart for God and for ministry. They are key leaders in our church, and the Lord brought our lives together through a mutual friend. Brenda and I have had the opportunity to co-lead a small group. Keith and I have had many conversations about God's heart concerning ministry. Encouraging them as husband and wife and leaders in ministry through prayer and guidance blesses me. What an incredible privilege to help them grow in their love for each other, their love for God and their love for people. They also encourage me as they share openly their lives with me.

A younger friend once told me I had become like a mother to her. Let me tell you, that freaked me out. A mother? I was a hip, happening young single! I wasn't ready to hear it, so she didn't say anything else about it and neither did I. But one day God decided to bring it up again. An inner voice said to me, *I've called you to be her spiritual mother and I don't want you to send her away again.*

Whoa, I thought; *where did that come from?*

I sought affirmation for this possible encounter with God. I called my friend to plan a time to talk, and I asked her to pray about our upcoming conversation. Several months had gone by since her first remark. When we talked, I shared what I believed I'd heard from God. Her reply was, "Didn't you know you were like a mother to me?" I was dumbfounded. She hadn't changed her perception of me. So we pursued an intentional mother-daughter spiritual relationship, and the Lord has blessed it. We have walked together through many happy and difficult times.

I can vividly remember when I sensed God asking me to mentor a certain young man. I felt acquainted with his heart. It seemed he wanted to serve God with all of it, even in the midst of struggles. I'd known him for years as a boy growing into a godly young man. Now that I'd had a closer look at who he was, I wanted to spur him on to follow hard after the Lord. He seemed comfortable with me.

When it seemed that God was telling me to reach out and help nurture this young man's growth in the Lord, I wondered if I was hearing correctly. Would God really have me mentor a young man? So far my mentoring relationships had been only with women. I said, *OK, God, I'll call him, and if it's really you, he'll respond positively.* I nervously dialed his number and told him what I thought was going on. His eager "Yes!" warmed my heart. We set up a time to begin right then, and this young man, Rick Cobb, became my spiritual son. Yes! God met us over and over again as Rick made himself vulnerable to the Lord and me. And what a joy he and his wife Trish are. Their one-year-old son Campbell is affectionately getting to know me as Auntie Skip, and he's my "hunk of love." I love it! Rick and Trish are now also proud parents of a new son, Landon Burnett. So I have another nephew to love on. God is good!

Relationships aren't always easy, but I'm blessed with a healthy number of people who love me, and I praise God for them. Contrary to what we might think, relationships don't just happen. We determine to what extent we allow others in. For the sake of spiritual and emotional health, it's wise to evaluate from time to time our relationships and adjust them accordingly. This process takes time, practice and hard work, but it pays off to be intentional.

Ask yourself these questions in evaluating your relationships:

- Where does your relationship stand?
- Is it mutually encouraging?
- Is it honest?
- Are you free to be yourself?
- Is it mutually giving?
- Do any areas need confronting?
- What changes would you like to see in the relationship?
- Ask each other, "What do we need to do for the continued growth of our relationship?

Granted, these questions may need alterations if you're clearly in a helping relationship with someone. We strive to extend grace in allowing another person room to grow.

FINDING THE RIGHT RELATIONSHIPS

I asked Kassandra, an administrative assistant to a single minister, her thoughts on intimacy. She had this to say:

> I don't have many deep friendships, but the ones I do have are blessed of God. Individuals who speak life into me and vice versa have developed into deeper friendships. I have pulled back from friends who tend to draw the life out of me, but I still love them in the Lord. I must also be mindful of the friendships I develop because of my position as an administrative assistant to our minister. I have found that some sisters have gotten close to me to get close to him. One relationship turned out to be disastrous. Overall, I tend to choose the God-chasers over the husband-chasers.

Kassandra is a wise woman in her relationships.

Jesus as our example will lead and guide us through his Holy Spirit into the right relationships. Left to ourselves, we would be intertwined with one unhealthy person after another. I'm thankful for the day I relinquished this area of my life to God. I had worn myself out trying to find and establish relationships. I now leave it up to the Lord to show me his will. Trusting him with the people of my world has brought me joy and freedom.

QUESTIONS FOR REFLECTION OR DISCUSSION

1. How did Leslee's story of intimacy affect you?

2. How would you define intimacy?

3. How have you experienced intimacy breakers in your relationships?

4. What experiences have you had with unsafe people? With safe people?

5. How do you develop intimacy in your relationships?

6. Do you have a soul friend? What is that like for you?

7. Describe your biological and spiritual family. In what ways can you improve on these relationships?

8. How do you respond to the idea that God provides ultimate intimacy?

Hooked on Relationships

I got the broom and went after my dad. I was five years old. My mom and dad were arguing, and at that early age, I stood up for my mom. My parents broke the argument and began laughing as my dad ran from the broom. Mom said, "We were just playing!" It didn't look like playtime in my little mind. So I took action!

My parents' relationship was strained, and most of the time I saw my father as the bad guy. I deplored the way he treated my mother. I desperately wanted to make the situation better, but I felt helpless. Mom used to tell me about the tender times my dad and I shared when I was a little girl, but by high school I hated him. She tried hard to fill in the gap between us and never spoke against him. But I witnessed his behavior and formed my own conclusions.

Before I finished high school, God interrupted my life and dealt with my attitude about my dad. I realized my hatred was wrong and had to go. The Holy Spirit began to show me that my dad was operating out of what he knew and helped me start focusing on the good he offered. As hard as this was, I practiced it. Slowly, my heart softened and the hatred subsided. My heart still grieved over my parents' relationship, but I was learning to deal with it in a healthier way, accepting the fact that it wasn't my marriage.

Although things improved between my dad and me, my pattern of fixing and rescuing was established, along with an unhealthy need to please people. These codependent tendencies followed me for years through my relationships.

Singles face twin dangers: one is not being connected enough, which we explored in the last chapter. The other danger is becoming overinvolved in people's lives.

STRUGGLING WITH CODEPENDENCY

My quest to fix, rescue and please others for their approval was an ongoing attempt to gain a sense of belonging and adequacy. Having grown up as an only child who didn't date much and had no best friend for years, I wanted to belong to someone other than my parents. I tried hard to make people love me. And when they didn't love and accept me the way I wanted them to, I was not happy.

With a nonexistent dating life, friendships were of the utmost importance to me. I poured myself into them with a frenzied urgency. I would wear others and myself out by being clingy and trying to meet my friends' every need. Unfortunately, this sometimes led to codependent relationships. I felt trapped and needy. Often my moodiness overtook me to the point where I could hardly stand myself. The root of codependency was deep, but God was able to pull it out.

The beginning of the end of my codependent lifestyle came with Shondraun, whom I met while working in the youth ministry of a church. Shondraun as a youth had her own struggles with belonging, and her family relationships were strained as well. She wanted my help and I wanted to give it, so I tried hard to be there for her, although her family didn't welcome my presence in her life because of my race. Soon my friendship with Shondraun began to consume a lot of my time. I didn't know how to send her away when I needed to focus on other issues. When her relationship with her parents became more strained because of me, I knew I had to break away. But it was tough. I asked myself how I could justify abandoning the relationship when I loved and cared for Shondraun. I was walking in a difficult place. But God in his graciousness gave me the strength to let go and trust him to take care of Shondraun without my help. I had to realize that I was not her savior.

I lessened the initiative I took to make contact with her. I wrote a letter outlining the problems in the relationship. I requested we have no further contact via phone or visits. I asked that she respond to the letter only if something was unclear (in my mind the letter was quite clear). Nevertheless, she called after receiving the letter and acted as if nothing was wrong. At this point, I had to verbally tell her that contact must be broken. She adhered. Years went by and Shondraun called again. After a sleepless night of prayer, I called her the next day and asked her to never call my house again. I've since moved with a different phone number. I don't know if she ever tried to call again. After that time, we saw each other at a store a distance from my home. We greeted each other warmly and kept going.

About a year after no contact with Shondraun, I began a book study with a friend on *Codependency: Emerging from the Eclipse* by Pat Springle. What an eye opener! I discovered that I had suffered from this problem all my life. How kind God was to minister to me as I sought to minister to my friend. "Wow," I said to her one day. "This is what I was, but I didn't know what to call it." I was shocked and grateful to God for meeting me in the pages of that book. After finishing it, I had somewhat of a vision. It was as though the Lord said, *I've delivered you from codependency. I've put a thick steel door between you and it, and if you try to go back there, you'll bump into the door and break your nose.* I visualized the thick steel door, and I can still see it in my mind today.

Since then I've turned toward that door a few times, bumped my nose and remembered. I've responded accordingly by putting that particular relationship in check. I'm thankful that these friendships are healthy to this day. Praise God for his faithfulness. He's helped me learn the difference between genuine caring and the need to be needed.

My friend Erin can identify. She's been on both sides of the invisible codependency fence.

We're told to love our friends and neighbors and that love always trusts. But are we supposed to trust in our friends and neighbors? We're told to hope in God, but are we ever to hope in people? We're foolish to say we don't need another part of the body of Christ, but are we to carry our own burdens?

In college when I fell in love with Jesus by responding to his love for me, many kind, godly brothers and sisters in Christ surrounded me. They spent time loving and teaching me. When we went different ways, I was broken-hearted—I had come to expect more of their time. Christians who are growing from newborns to maturity can become codependent on the people loving them, and that's what had happened to me. Disciplers are wise to remember that the goal of discipling a new Christian is to teach them sole dependence on Jesus while learning to carry their burdens and the burdens of others. I don't see these goals as mutually exclusive.

I continue to learn not to have unhealthy expectations of people. I am practicing having no expectations of friends and family. This may sound depressing, but it's actually freeing. I want to be a faithful friend and love like God loves us, without expectation. I look forward to lots of fun time with my friends, but I don't want to freak out when God ordains less time with them than I wanted. I like to talk to Christ about it: "Jesus, whatever good thing I think I need from these people—time, help or affection—I know I really need it from you. Somehow, please fill my emptiness with your love directly or even from within the body of Christ."

SINGLE CHRISTIANS AND THE CODEPENDENCY TRAP

Single adults sometimes feel desperate for special care and attention. When asked what they dislike about singleness, many women respond, "Not belonging. Not having a loving husband in my bed every night. Having to make big decisions on my own." Or, "I constantly struggle to separate my singleness from the thought that something is wrong with me. I don't like not feeling cherished by a man. I feel alone. I hate coming home to an empty house."

Getting involved with others makes us feel less lonely, so we often attempt to care for people in order to fill our own emptiness. That's what I did. Christ tells us to deny ourselves, but as a codependent Christian I didn't know how to interpret that in a healthy way. For me, denying myself became another way of enabling, fixing and not having an identity. Like many codependent Christians, I carried the "oughts" and "shoulds" of society and my faith on my own shoulders. The load is oppressive and indicates a wrong perspective of Christ and the Christian life. But in the context of singleness, differentiating between codependency and Christian caring is difficult.

Codependent behavior may look other-focused, but in reality it is self-focused: I care for you so you will care for me, accept me, vali-

---

HOLDING ON TO JESUS

I have learned that I am greatly valued, deeply loved and accepted by God. And out of this understanding, I am able to exercise real self-denial and real commitment to Christ. Now that I understand codependency, I can look at the fruit of the Spirit in Galatians 5 or the love chapter in 1 Corinthians 13 and apply it in my daily interactions with others in a holistic way.

date me. The overcommitted drive of codependency may even resemble a deep commitment to Christ. Codependents actually make the best employees and church workers because of their effectiveness, loyalty and intenseness. But while Christian commitment and codependency can seem similar on the outside, on the inside they are leagues apart.

In true caring relationships, we look after ourselves as we look after others. We don't substitute others' needs for our own. We are responsible for living life to the fullest even while we help others do the same. If we find ourselves taking care of others more than we take care of ourselves, that signals a problem. We're becoming too enmeshed in the world of others; we're losing objectivity. To avoid this, we need to keep a healthy perspective of our worth and value before God. Therefore, in the end, we are both nourished and helped.

Lisa knows all too well the devastating results of codependency. Her relationship with Dwight was the first dysfunctional relationship she'd had with a man since becoming a Christian. Although Lisa had never thought of dating anyone at her church, Dwight, a minister there, asked for her phone number and invited her to dinner. After that date, they started to spend time together.

During the first month of their friendship, Lisa and Dwight mostly talked about things of the Lord. However, after he started coming to her house, they progressed to a romantic relationship. Problems soon appeared.

> The way he was living didn't line up with what he was professing. He was needy, jealous and a compulsive liar. He told people in the church that he'd been living with me and that we'd traveled outside the country, neither of which was true. He had an inferiority complex and lied to make himself look good.

Dwight treated Lisa so badly that her friends asked her why she remained in the relationship. I asked her the same question.

He kept saying that the Lord told him I was to be his wife. I kept thinking, "Well, maybe I'm not hearing from the Lord." But I couldn't see marriage happening, even though we were sexually involved. I was scared to believe him and scared not to believe him. My behavior showed the state of my spiritual life. If my relationship with the Lord had been strong, I would have known that Dwight's presence in my life was not of God. I would not have relied on Dwight to hear from God for me. I was trying hard to make things OK by staying with him.

Everything was telling me not to trust Dwight from the first time I met him, but maybe because I'd gotten used to the company, I let my guard down and lost sight of my real desires. I kept thinking, "I'm crazy. There's nothing wrong with this guy. He's a man of God." Yet we were involved in sexual sin.

I finally saw the relationship for what it was. The biggest turning point in my decision to walk away was realizing his true character. I got physically ill when I talked to him. I was so stressed by the relationship that my back started aching. I finally realized there was nothing I could do to make the relationship work, so I ended it.

I wish I had waited before even entering the relationship. God would have shown me what I needed to know beforehand. But I opened the door for the devil to come in. I don't fault Dwight. I fault myself for not listening to the voice of warning about him. Oh, if only we would wait for God to reveal his will to us in our relationships!

Lisa learned some hard but valuable lessons through her relationship with Dwight. She's now dating a previous boyfriend, and the relationship is going well. Instead of repeating past mistakes, she wants to learn from them and develop healthy relationships with men.

WAITING FOR THE LORD

We can learn to wait on God in any relationship. He'll let us know how we can best care for others. He'll let us know when to initiate a friendship and when to wait for the other person to do so. He'll help us see how much space to give people so we don't smother or stifle them. Sometimes we think we want what's best for someone so much that we move into a controlling mode. Our intentions may be good, but somewhere along the way we become selfish. We try to fix people to look and act the way we think they should. At this point, we cross that person's boundary line. We need to learn to respect the boundaries of others while helping them to respect ours.

Left to ourselves, we would destroy one another, but the Lord is faithful to help us learn how to love from a pure heart. We can look to Jesus Christ in the Gospels as our model for healthy patterns of interacting with people. For example, Jesus loved the rich young ruler but let him walk away. He didn't beg him to reconsider or offer to cut him a deal to make discipleship easier (Luke 18:18-27). And in John 21, we see Jesus' love and acceptance of Peter after Peter denied him three times (John 21:15-19).

Also, because his Holy Spirit indwells us, he will teach us the truth of Christ and empower us to live life more and more like him (John 16:13-15). Trying to relate well with others takes a lot of work. And honestly, if I didn't love Jesus, I wouldn't put forth as much effort. But, I'm mindful of I John 4:20 which says, "If someone says, 'I love God,' and hates his brother, he is a liar; for the one who does not love his brother whom he has seen, cannot love God whom he has not seen."

Psalm 66:16-20 reflects my heart as I think of all God does to help me relate as best I can with others.

Come and hear, all who fear God,
And I will tell of what He has done for my soul.
I cried to Him with my mouth,

And He was extolled with my tongue.
If I regard wickedness in my heart,
The Lord will not hear;
But certainly God has heard;
He has given heed to the voice of my prayer.
Blessed be God,
Who has not turned away my prayer
Nor His lovingkindness from me.

Praise God that he doesn't expect us to live life by ourselves. He promises to lead and guide us in the way that we should go and to counsel us with his eye upon us (Psalm 32:8). I'm thankful that he never gave up on me, didn't leave me in the pit of my pitiful attempts to meet my needs through other people. He patiently waited until I would seek him first with my whole heart, and I praise him with my whole heart for it. Truly, my heart belongs to Jesus.

QUESTIONS FOR REFLECTION OR DISCUSSION

1. How would you define codependency?
2. What's your reaction to the story about Shondraun?
3. In what ways can you identify with the characteristics of codependency?
4. How do you interpret "deny yourself"?
5. What can you learn from Lisa's relationship with Dwight?
6. Which relationships are you struggling with right now? What help do you need?

To Date or Not to Date

Here's how one Christian brother expressed his frustration with the dating scene as he saw it: "Why do the good guys finish last? What's the attraction to bad boys? The good guys are the last ones chosen. Then when we're picked, we're left to deal with all the baggage the women carry from dating the bad boys in the first place."

I think this young man is asking some good questions. It's time for women to ask themselves the same thing.

SHOULD I DATE?

So what's all the hoopla about dating? Some enjoy it; others are heartbroken by it. These days I've noticed two primary schools of thought. One says dating is right, good and necessary. The other says dating is not a good thing. Joshua Harris's book *I Kissed Dating Goodbye* encapsulates the argument against dating. I'm not biased either way, but I must admit I liked his chapter titled "The Seven Habits of Highly Defective Dating." He states:

1. Dating leads to intimacy but not necessarily to commitment.

2. Dating tends to skip the "friendship" stage of a relationship.

3. Dating often mistakes a physical relationship for love.

4. Dating often isolates a couple from other vital relationships.

5. Dating in many cases distracts young adults from their primary responsibility of preparing for the future.

6. Dating can cause discontentment with God's gift of singleness.

7. Dating creates an artificial environment for evaluating another person's character.

Joshua Harris recommends a courtship approach, which moves from friendship and relating in group contexts to a formal engagement without dating.

On the other hand, Stacy and Paula Rinehart in their book *Choices: Finding God's Way in Dating, Sex, Singleness, and Marriage* give these reasons for dating:

1. to develop socially

2. to have a good time

3. greater commonality

4. potential for genuine acceptance

5. freedom from expectations

6. to grow in Christ.

And M. Blaine Smith in his book *Should I Get Married?* says, "Dating can be done with integrity. Christians who determine to do so can navigate the challenging waters of dating without compromising their values and without being damaged for life. And they can through this process find someone suitable for them to marry."

So, considering all this, should single Christian women date? The answer is not a simple yes or no but begins with trying to understand what the Lord wants us to do and how we can please him. As we see ourselves through God's eyes, we're more likely to look at this issue from his perspective. As we seek him with a clean heart through Scripture and prayer, committed to doing his will, he will answer. Thinking wisely breeds good choices. We need to pray and search the Scriptures to discern God's will for our lives.

If you decide that dating is the path you will take, then the most important question is, who should you date?

Avoiding Mr. Wrong

There's one tried and true method that will help you avoid Mr. Wrong: only date someone you would consider marrying. Stephen Arterburn and Dr. Meg Rinck in their book *Avoiding Mr. Wrong (and What to Do If You Didn't)* present a gallery of ten men who will ruin your life. Unfortunately, I've seen these men come into women's lives over and over again. Of the ten listed, I've seen Mr. Wonderful, the Control Freak and the Angry Man in operation the most. When I think of Mr. Wonderful, Louis comes to mind. Like a tornado, he touched down into the life of my girlfriend, swept her up, and before I knew it put a ring on her finger. I couldn't believe my eyes as I watched it happen. And obviously, as her friend I had to let her go. I was leery of Mr. Wonderful, but I couldn't live someone else's life. And as is often the case, he turned out to be not so Mr. Wonderful. And although she has beautiful children, she has a scarred heart to go with them.

The Control Freak reminds me of Terry. Even though Terry was a control freak with his wife Madge, his insecurities dripped all over the place. He always maintained separate banking accounts. He made sure that she was on a very limited budget, restraining her from doing anything creative and on her own. I watched Madge try to fill in the gap on numerous occasions. She was so eager to help him be happy and he took full advantage of it. I watched Madge wait on her husband hand and foot. She says, "When we got married, I thought we could help each other become better. Instead he was interested in maintaining his old habits." I had to practice holding my tongue a lot! Once again, it wasn't my marriage; it was hers.

And then there's the Angry Man, who is so pent up with insecurities and the need for control that he's a time bomb waiting to go off. Although he tries to hold it together for the sake of appearances, his anger leaks out all too often in public. Lucy dated an Angry Man whose rage took the form of physical and emotional abuse. I helped

Lucy escape from Michael and his violence, but she was so entrenched in his world that she returned. I was heartbroken by the news. May God help us, and may we listen to him, as he guides us to the person who will help us become more like him.

FINDING MR. RIGHT

Tonya is a twenty-six-year-old single Christian woman who has dated only non-Christian men in the past. But in the last four years she hasn't dated anyone. During this waiting period, she's formed some conclusions about the kind of man she would like to date in the future. She has this to say:

> I now see the importance of dating a Christian. In previous relationships I wasn't growing as I should have been; I wasn't nurtured. Those relationships were one-sided and I felt taken advantage of. I did things my way and they didn't work.
>
> Now I want someone by God's design and plan. I want to date someone who has a good relationship with him and who is a spiritual leader. I would like someone intelligent, with interests and hobbies. Someone with a sense of humor would be nice since I like to laugh. He would show how important I am to him by his sensitivity to my needs. He wouldn't be so focused on his needs that he neglected mine.
>
> A confident man appeals to me—someone who can stand on his own two feet and doesn't need a mother. I'm attracted to a man who is goal-oriented and purpose-driven. I want someone with a personality, someone who gets along well with a number of different people in social situations. As far as physical characteristics, the one that matters most is that he's tall.

How's your prayer life? There's no way to know who God wants us to date without asking him. There are a lot of con artists out there who would like to deceive us into thinking they're someone they're not. Praying for discernment helps us spot these charlatans so we don't give them the time of day. Trusting God's wisdom with the intent to obey helps us see clearly and keep ourselves open to the Holy Spirit's scrutiny.

Also, choose carefully the characteristics of the kind of man you're interested in. Make that list and check it more than twice, especially if you're dating someone. By keeping abreast of your list, you will more easily spot red flags in the person you're dating. You may also detect positive qualities that weren't on your list—those are a bonus!

Next, seek wise counsel. Don't hide your dating relationship from people whose insight you value. If you feel like you need to hide him, that's an indication that something's wrong. Friends and family can't live your life for you, but they may see things that you can't. Keep yourself accountable.

In another book, *Finding Mr. Right*, authors Arterburn and Rinck offer insight into the kind of man who is a desirable potential mate. Mr. Right is a man of character, faith and purpose. He is confident in

HOLDING ON TO JESUS

Blessed are the poor in spirit, for theirs is the kingdom of heaven.

Blessed are those who mourn, for they shall be comforted.

Blessed are the gentle, for they shall inherit the earth.

Blessed are those who hunger and thirst for righteousness, for they shall be satisfied.

Blessed are the merciful, for they shall receive mercy.

Blessed are the pure in heart, for they shall see God.

Blessed are the peacemakers, for they shall be called sons of God.

MATTHEW 5:3-9

who he is in Christ. The trademark of his character and purpose is his faith. Despite the fact that Christian values such as the ones Jesus describes in the Beatitudes (Matthew 5) are not seen as manly in our culture, Mr. Right is loving, compassionate, gentle and tender. The world sees these qualities as weakness, but they actually exude strength. God uses these characteristics in a man to reach the world.

Mr. Right also loves laughter and learning. Although he doesn't have to be the life of the party, he enjoys life. As he trusts God to unfold the plan for his life, he learns to make the most of every day. He's not stuck in his past but looks expectantly into the future. Praise God for men who are not afraid to honor God wherever they are—relationships, work, home and play. Another important quality: Mr. Right doesn't put women down, and he's secure enough as a person to enjoy the company and leadership of strong women. I pray that more of our Christian men will become established in their faith to the point that Christ has free rein in their lives. We sisters will benefit greatly as that happens.

One day when I was talking with my friend Fay about Mr. Right, she gave some good insights:

> First and foremost I want a man who loves the Lord. I want someone who is honest, has integrity, is dependable and has a sense of humor. I'd like someone who's not afraid to show his softer side and knows that it's OK for a man to cry sometimes. It's not a given that you can find a true Christian man in the church. If you're not careful, you can be duped. Some men flock to the church hoping to find nice women, but their intentions aren't honorable. They can talk the talk and quote Scripture eloquently, but if they're not the real deal, eventually their true self will emerge.
>
> I met Joe and he knew what I was about—that I was a Christian woman who liked to go to church and didn't drink. So he

said he loved going to church and he loved the Lord too. We agreed to be friends and get to know each other. I told him I wasn't interested in a sexual relationship, and he said he understood. But after only a few weeks he started making the moves sexually. For me, that was a turnoff. He'd back off and then try again. Eventually I said, "I told you I'm not interested in that." And that was the end of it.

My word to women is to stand your ground. The quickest way to lose someone is to compromise yourself. Don't say one thing and then do another. I know it's hard to wait, especially if you've been sexually active before, but waiting this time will be worth it. We may fall down, but we can get back up by God's grace and strength. Look to the Lord to help you.

I appreciate Fay's testimony and I'm thankful for the men I've met who, unlike Joe, display aspects of Mr. Right. I assure you that when I'm around these men, I encourage them strongly to keep running the race well.

GOING OUT EVERY NIGHT?

So we've covered the process of deciding whether we're in a spiritually appropriate place for dating and the qualities to look for in the men we date. But our discernment doesn't stop there. We also need to decide how much time we will dedicate to the dating process. Should we go out once a week? Every night? Are weeknights OK or should we stick to weekends? Our answer will depend on individual preferences, other commitments in our lives and the leading of the Holy Spirit. As we stay open and honest with God, we can determine a healthy amount of time to spend with the person.

In order to decide how much time to invest, we need to evaluate the health of the relationship. To do this, we can ask ourselves these questions:

- Are we both growing and learning from each other?
- Do we have each other's best interest in mind?
- Am I showing forth Christ's love and is he showing it to me?
- Are we enjoying each other or dragging each other down?

Answering these questions honestly helps us make the most of our time instead of wasting it.

ARE YOU THE RIGHT KIND OF WOMAN?

The authors of the book *Finding Mr. Right* also spend some time describing Miss Right, because we can't expect to build healthy relationships if our own house isn't in order. Miss Right is approachable, moderate, genuine, spiritually committed, wise, playful, fun and relaxed. She is open to meeting and getting to know a man without flinging herself all over him. Now that I think about it, Miss Right is a lot like a friend of mine. This friend has gone through many hard lessons, but I see evidence in her of the refining process. She is alive and vibrant in a new way. As she gains confidence in what God is doing in her life, it shows all over her face and the way she carries herself.

Miss Right is genuine and authentic. What you see is what you get. Her focus is on Christ foremost; she seeks him above all else and wants to please him first. With her eyes on Christ, Miss Right trusts him to provide her best in every area of life. Struggle she may sometimes, but she is growing in her faith most of the time and her commitment to Christ is evident.

Miss Right is wise. She responds to wisdom's cry in Proverbs 2—which, by the way, personifies wisdom as feminine!

> For if you cry for discernment,
> Lift your voice for understanding;
> If you seek her as silver
> And search for her as for hidden treasures;

Then you will discern the fear of the LORD
And discover the knowledge of God. (Proverbs 2:3-5)

Miss Right seeks to exercise this wisdom in every encounter with men. She doesn't shut off her perceptory faculties out of desperation but interacts with all antennae fully operational. She senses when she's in danger and when it's OK to continue in a relationship. Her eyes are alert, her ears are attentive, she smells insincerity and she's careful about the touch she receives. She is not perfect, but she pursues wisdom with vigilance.

Miss Right is playful, fun and relaxed. She knows how to have a God-honoring good time. She loves laughter and knows that without a sense of fun, she tends to get stuck thinking "woe is me." Her life is not perfect, but she's able to let go of hardship and disappointment and move on. She reminds her girlfriends to lighten up and give themselves a break. She's learned through walking with God that he has a great sense of humor, and when she can't help but laugh at circumstances, she's pretty sure he joins in.

Miss Right has a life of her own. She develops interests and skills of her own and is not focused solely on relationships with men. She maintains balance in her life. My friend Kelly is a perfect example. Kelly is not dating anyone, and though she has met a few interesting men, she's willing to wait for God's best. In the meantime, she's continuing her education in grad school and has just bought a home. She plays sports and attends Bible study. Her faith in Christ shines all over her radiant and exuberant face. Her zest for life encourages everyone she meets.

WHEN SHOULD I SAY NO?

Most single women I've met desire male companionship of some type. Sometimes it's such a strong desire that it's hard to say no to poor relationships. Others of us find it difficult to say no because of shyness, a fear of rejection, feelings of guilt or not wanting to hurt someone's feelings. We sometimes fall into the trap of people pleasing or wanting to date for the recognition it brings. Or it could simply be that we want to date someone because we really care for him even though we know a relationship would not be right. We want to say yes when we need to say no.

My friend Corrinne knows all too well what can happen when we're ambivalent about saying yes or no. She and Joey, a nonbeliever at her workplace, had decided to spend some time together as friends, just hanging out and getting to know each other. Corrinne wondered how this would work. Could she keep it as just friends or would she find herself involved emotionally? She knew it was up to her to guard her heart. She says:

> Eventually he wrote me a card that said he really liked me. My reaction was, "Oh, shoot!" We talked and I told him that I needed him to stay away for a while. And he did. It was a hard decision, especially considering the void I'd been experiencing with God. I'd had a hard time communicating with him and was not hearing him like I used to. Now I'd lost this great friend who was special, and I didn't feel like God had shown up either. But as I put forth the effort to seek God more diligently, I felt like he began to heal my life and my friendship with Joey. I finally seemed to be hearing from God.
>
> One day at work Joey came by to say hi. Soon we began to spend time together again. On one hand I felt OK about it, but on the other I didn't have the reassurance in my feelings that it was all right. And that's where I am now—in the middle of it. I'm frustrated with myself because I've never been attracted to anyone who wasn't a Christian. I've always said I wouldn't even consider it. But now that I have this special relationship with a non-Christian, it feels too good for me to say no.

I'm not following what I know is the wisest path, and I'm worried that my love for Jesus might not win out. I've wondered how far God would let me go with this. I've never really pushed the boundaries of my life. I've wanted to do the right thing, but right now I feel like I'm playing with it. I've asked if there is any way around being unequally yoked with Joey. I feel like Eve when the serpent said, "Surely God didn't say it or mean it this way." I can see what's happening.

I felt Corrinne's heartache as she shared with me, knowing that her story is not new or unique. Other Christian women have the same struggle, whether new to the faith or seasoned believers. Many women by nature tend to be people pleasers, so it can be very difficult to have non-Christian friendships and not let them go too far. And although friendship with nonbelievers is important, jeopardizing our standards in dating can be disastrous.

At times Christians, men and women, fall into the trap of missionary dating. Thinking they are strong enough to draw a nonbeliever to Christ, they enter and remain in a relationship with that person. But too often the opposite happens. The Christian loses her grip on the faith and lowers her standards. A misplaced desire for evangelism is a dangerous thing in a dating relationship. We can't take this reality too seriously.

In 2 Corinthians 6:14 we read that we are not to be "bound together with unbelievers," and Amos 3:3 says, "Can two people walk together without agreeing on the direction?" (NLT). When Christ is not the center of our dating relationship, we are caught in a tug-of-war between pleasing the unbeliever and pleasing God. We find that our desire for the things of God slowly erodes. The enemy is sneaky and lulls us into being deceived. We wake up one day, deeply entangled in a wrong relationship, and ask, what happened? Similarly, beware of those who make conversions of convenience, those who say yes to Christ so they can be with you. Rely on the Spirit of God to help you discern this type of person.

WHAT ABOUT INTERRACIAL DATING?

I had a discussion once with a white high school girl who was pregnant with a young black man's baby. As we talked, she shared that she was rebelling against her parents by being in this relationship. I questioned her rationale in getting back at her parents in this way, but she said she loved the young man. I wondered if this were true, considering the tension with her parents. I grieved for the unborn child who would enter into such conflict.

An article in the magazine *Christian Single* titled "The Color Factor" offers several factors for interracial couples to consider.

- First, see the big picture. Assess the overall compatibility of your relationship. The more similarities you share, the more likely it is that your relationship will be a success.

- Second, consider your extended family. Family attitudes play a big part in relationships, whether we want to admit it or not.

- Third, test your motives. Why are you entering into a mixed dating relationship? What is true of any couple is especially true of interracial couples. To have a healthy relationship, both individuals must be emotionally stable.

- Fourth, think of future children. Will you be putting your children under undue duress because of the marriage?

Marcia Hollins, who has been in an interracial marriage for thirty-one years, says, "If you put doubt and fear and racism into your children you'll get that. If you instill love and a Christlike perspective, you'll get that. We believe our children got the best of both worlds." A wonderful resource for understanding multiracial children is Sundee Frazier's book *Check All That Apply: Finding Wholeness as a Multiracial Person*. I've learned a lot from Sundee. She describes her upbringing and early adult years as the daughter of one black parent and one white parent.

WHAT IF HE'S SHORT?

It's important to have godly standards for dating—even rigid requirements when it comes to areas of morality and Christian commitment. However, there are some superficial areas where we need to be open to God and compromise. Do you have preferences about height, weight or hair color? Most of us do. But be careful not to close your mind and heart to a good man who might be physically different from what you expected. For example, consider the experience my friend Maile had with the "height factor":

> I am two and a half inches taller than Scott. It was a bit of a struggle for both of us in the beginning of our dating relationship and a while for me after marriage. Nevertheless, it actually turned out to be a blessing. Since Scott was shorter and younger than me (by a year and a half), I didn't think about him as a potential mate. I just got to know him as a friend. We attended a prayer meeting together for well over a year before we ever had a real "date."
>
> I wore high heels to church one day. As I stood beside him I felt very tall and awkward. However, it didn't stop the relationship from progressing and eventually we got married. But even after that I struggled with Scott being shorter than me and weighing only little more. This fueled an eating disorder because I was determined not to weigh more than Scott. I wanted to feel small next to my husband and to feel that he was big and protective. It took quite a while for me to accept Scott's height.
>
> Scott's main struggle took place before he ever asked me out. He realized that if it weren't for my height and age, I would be the girl he'd want to marry. God took Scott to Isaiah 53 and

showed him that Jesus' appearance was not desirable either. God seemed to open Scott's eyes to see that physical appearance doesn't matter. Scott says that I make him feel taller and that when people see us, they probably average our heights unconsciously. Now the height difference is a special uniqueness to us. We like to laugh and joke about it.

How Do I Find Him?

When it comes to knowing where to meet Mr. Right, there are two schools of thought. One says we should position ourselves to meet eligible men by attending singles groups, serving at church, using dating services, or going on blind dates arranged by people we trust. The other side tells us to let God bring along the people he wants us to spend time with as we carry on with day-to-day living. We remain open, but we don't actively search. You will need to prayerfully decide how God wants you to approach this question.

A friend of mine met a man through a dating service. Although I personally am a little leery of the idea of online romance, I agree with my friend's advice if you do choose this method of "dating":

> I would caution anyone considering using the Internet as a dating tool to be *very* careful. Anyone vulnerable can be deceived by flirtatious words and ego-boosting talk. Read everything you can get your hands on about following Gods' teaching. Arm yourself with the Word of God so you will know when someone is handing you a line. Remember that God wants us to be content in whatever state we find ourselves in.

How Long Should I Date?

Once we're in a dating relationship that we believe is right and possibly moving toward marriage, the next step is deciding how long to date before engagement. How do we know what's long enough? Most experts unquestionably say that the length of the dating relationship is the largest factor in discerning if you're both ready for marriage. In *The Ten Commandments of Dating,* Ben Young and Samuel Adams are "convinced that the No. 1 reason couples divorce is not money, sex, or infidelity, but rather a hasty decision to get married."

Author and marriage counselor Neil Clark Warren suggests that couples date for two years to decide if marriage is the next step. He says, "Most relationships are focused on romance in the first year, and very little 'painful truth' becomes available until near the end of that first year." According to Warren, about 47 percent of marriages now end with "mutual incompatibility" as the stated reason, and Young says that dating should be a long-term process of determining whether that compatibility exists. Yet practically speaking, not everyone needs two years to discern God's will. If both individuals are growing in their relationship with God and each other, they are better equipped than an expert to decide if God is leading them toward marriage.

Someone recently asked me a good question: "If you didn't believe God was directly calling you to consider marriage, would you date?" My answer is that while I'm interested in friendship with men, I would not pursue a dating relationship. I would enjoy doing fun things with my male friends, discussing the things of the Lord and encouraging each other's faith. But I'm not interested in a commitment other than friendship. Of course, the bottom line is God's will for my life. If one day he decides he wants me to marry, I'm confident he'll make that clear. But I have to admit that I often thank him for my singleness and remind him that I would like to die a single woman.

Scripture gives ample insight on relationships, as Psalm 19 reminds us: "God's Word warns us of danger and directs us to hidden treasure. Otherwise how will we find our way? Or know when we play the fool?" (Psalm 19:11-12 *The Message*). As we search the Scriptures, seek wise counsel, stay honest with God and ourselves, and pray, I believe the answer will become clear. Often when a decision seems fuzzy, it's because we really don't want to hear what God has to say. We claim that we don't know what his will is, and we sway. We're tossed and turned. But God doesn't play games with us. If we turn to him and seek to honor him, he makes our path clear and straight.

QUESTIONS FOR REFLECTION OR DISCUSSION

1. What is your reaction to the statement in the first paragraph, "The good guys are the last ones chosen"?

2. Do you think people should date? Explain.

3. If you're interested in dating, who do you think are acceptable people to date?

4. What are your thoughts about the various descriptions of Mr. Wrong?

5. What has been your experience with 2 Timothy 3:6-7?

6. Which description of Mr. Right appeals to you most?

7. Discuss reasons why women in particular have a hard time saying no. Respond to Corrinne's story.

8. How do the characteristics of Miss Right make you feel?

9. Which school of thought do you agree with in how to date?

Dealing with Day-to-Day Responsibilities

Singleness is, to put it mildly, a challenging way to live. Without a good support system, single adults can easily fall into loneliness and despair. One of the most common reasons why people want to get married is the companionship of having someone to share life with. I remember one of my single colleagues in ministry who once commented, "The married men in my circle have their wives to help them. They do their laundry, cook and help with other needs. As single adults, we do it all alone."

Teresa, a forty-two-year-old single Christian woman, shares these sentiments. "It gets very lonely sometimes," she says. "I miss the companionship. Having one income is hard; there are no extras after the bills are paid. There's no handyman to move things or do minor repairs. I have to practice celibacy. There's no one to spend the holidays with other than family members."

There's no doubt about it. Singleness is a tough row to hoe, especially if you're not single by choice. But with God's grace and some attention to practical life skills, it doesn't have to be overwhelming. In fact, it can be a vibrant, full and rewarding lifestyle.

FINANCES

Handling financial matters as single adults has both pros and cons. We get to call the shots, but we also have to shoulder the responsibilities. I've met a lot of poor money managers in my day—and I used to be one of them. I admit I was spoiled growing up and never learned to manage my finances well. I'm still working at it and trusting God to help me become a good steward. I read books on financial management and attend workshops, and I'm learning to apply what I learn. It helps for me to remember that the Lord owns everything and has entrusted me to care for some of it. I also try to maintain a grateful attitude, which motivates me to make better decisions.

The Lord got my friend Lanore's attention through the book *Rich Dad, Poor Dad* by Robert Kiyosaki. He challenged her to utilize her resources in a new way by starting a women's investment club. She says:

> Through this book I realized I was getting poorer each day that I worked. I wanted to understand more about the world of investing, and I believed an investment club would be a great opportunity for others like myself to get together and learn about investing, finances and money matters. And prayerfully we would make a little money in the process.
>
> I chose an all-female club because most of the men in my immediate circle already knew a lot about investing. If there were men in the club, I knew it would be easy for me to give my monthly dues, let them do the research and make all the decisions without getting personally involved in the learning process. By having a club with others like myself, however, I would be forced to do research and learn, otherwise the club would fail. We bring in experts to help and give advice, but the ultimate decisions lie with the ladies of the club.
>
> In the investment club, I've learned how to research and evaluate stocks, bonds and mutual funds. I'm thankful for all that I'm learning, not just about finances, but also about establishing a successful organization.

When we look into financial opportunities, we can do our consciences and the world as much good as our bank accounts by considering socially responsible investments. This means putting our resources toward firms that help benefit society, are environmentally responsible, treat their workers well and don't manufacture harmful products such as tobacco or alcohol.

TRANSPORTATION

I miss my Dad's wisdom when it comes to cars. When he was around, Dad helped me purchase cars and gave helpful guidance with maintenance. After he was gone, Mom was also a great support, both financially and with advice. Although she didn't know much about how cars worked, she knew where to get the right kind of help.

Now I turn to others. My friend Barry helped me purchase my last car, Harmony. (That's my car's name.) I'd heard for years that women who purchase a car alone are often taken advantage of, so I enlisted Barry, who represented me well. We had discussed my needs, desires and resources beforehand. When we told the salesman what we were looking for and he told us what he could offer, Barry and I asked the salesman to leave so we could talk it over. Barry gave me his listening ear and wise counsel, and when the salesman reentered, we were ready to make a decision. Barry hung in there with me until midnight, when I drove my new Harmony home.

My friend Ann recently went through her own car saga, in which she witnessed God's provision numerous times:

> While driving to a family gathering on Christmas Eve, the transmission on my 1989 Toyota Corolla began to go. I was on a state highway and had no cell phone, so I prayed, "Lord, please let someone stop and help me!" As I pulled over to the side of the road, a couple driving behind me pulled over also, got out of their car and asked if they could help. They had heard

the sounds coming out of my engine. My reply was, "You are an answer to prayer!" I feel that God engineered this to happen on a state highway where someone would be more likely to stop than on a busy interstate.

With their help and knowledge of the area, I was able to get to a gas station and call my sister so she could pick me up. While waiting, I began to call around for a rental car because I needed to drive home Christmas evening. Of course, at 3 p.m. on Christmas Eve, car rental offices had already closed. When my sister arrived and we discussed this, she offered to let me drive her "extra vehicle"—a big Chevy Silverado truck! I continued to drive it for the next three weeks, so I didn't have to pay for a rental car.

God also provided a new car. A Christian mechanic friend of mine had a good friend, also a Christian, at a car dealership. This dealer began looking for a good used car for me and helped me connect with the vehicle I know God wanted me to have. God is a definitely a God of detail!

Cars can certainly be a source of stress. If the thought of car shopping and maintenance makes you break out in hives, there's nothing that says you absolutely have to own a car. For us as Americans this may seem unheard of, but in most cities it's possible to get around just fine using public transportation. Many places are easily accessible, and you may discover unexpected freedom without a car to maintain or payments to make. Just make sure, whatever your mode of transport, that you take precautions and exercise safety.

I'm thankful that God cares about our transportation needs. And although at times his provision may not be in the form of what we would like, he is faithful. I'm thankful too for a supportive community of friends who aid me with such needs.

FAMILY

As single adults, we sometimes have to deal with family expectations that don't match up with the reality of our lives. Some of us listen constantly to parents who complain about not having grandchildren. Others have to deal with well-meaning but misplaced attempts at matchmaking. Communicating with family can be difficult, but we still need to put forth the effort to interact effectively with our parents, siblings, aunts, uncles and cousins.

Michelle, a young single woman in my small group, does this well. She moved 450 miles away from her immediate family for a career opportunity, but it's obvious that she's close to them from the affectionate way she talks about them. Her family consists of her mother and her brother, who is eleven months older. Her father died when she was six. Michelle feels close to her family because of their trust, honesty and support:

> After my dad died, Mom decided she wanted her kids to live a life of Christianity. She wanted us to have values, to know our purpose and live productive lives. She felt that public schools would not give the entire picture, including God's Word, so we attended a Christian school to help in our spiritual growth.
>
> When I need help, my family assists me in finding a solution. Their love is active. Even strangers speak of how blessed I am to have a family like I have because of the way they care for others. My extended family consists of caregivers—doctors and nurses.
>
> As a single woman, my family helps me know I am not alone in making decisions. When I make decisions that seem to fail, my brother helps put them in a positive light and redirect my energy. I talk with my mom or brother daily for connection and to keep our communication open.

MEALS

Meals? What meals? I'm a single woman with a minute interest in cooking. Thank God for restaurants and for washed, bagged salad! In addition, God has blessed me richly with dear friends who cook well and are willing to share. My primary job growing up was learning how to clean. I was busy keeping the house spotless (not always by choice) while Mom worked in the kitchen preparing something fabulous. My Aunt Florrie is also a wonderful cook whose food I enjoy whenever I have the opportunity to do so.

On the other hand, my friend Jan has been cooking since she was twelve years old and baking since she was sixteen. Needless to say, I like having Jan around. Here's her story:

> I have always loved knowing that I could prepare something that would bring pleasure to those who ate it. Even in my youth, I was careful to prepare meals with a variety of colors because I wanted them to look pretty and taste good too. I had two aunts who could bake your socks off, and I always wanted to be as good as they were. As I got older, cooking became more social. I liked having people over and letting them sit down to a home-cooked meal, especially in college where most of my friends ate from the horrible student center café or fast food places.
>
> Now I'm passionate about learning how to cook in a way that promotes health or, at the very least, doesn't detract from it. I'm motivated to share all I've learned with others so they can eat familiar foods in a healthier way. My interest in health ministry began after witnessing the death of a dear friend who, after being diagnosed with ovarian cancer and given six months to live, actually died within three months.
>
> Since I have the gift of teaching, I wanted to share my knowledge with my Sunday school students and did so enthusiasti-

cally. Several people implemented dietary changes with noted health improvements.

Two years ago on Father's Day, my dad had the first of several strokes. My sister and I decided to research the effects of diet on stroke patients and suggest some of these changes to my mom, who prepares the meals for the household. My father, although reluctant, accepted the dietary changes. His health began to improve, as did that of other members of the household. It's a financial strain to provide the assistance needed for my parents, but quite frankly, if I'm going to struggle financially to pay a bill, I will certainly struggle to help my parents.

I'm energized by the prospect of bringing illumination to as many as would hear me. My heart's passion is to tell the world how to implement simple dietary changes that will improve overall health. I believe with all my heart that if you know better, you'll do better. Toward this end, I have also partnered with a dear friend and created BakeWorks, a bakery specializing in wholesome whole-grain products. I believe wholeheartedly that food can be good *for* you and still taste good *to* you, and our baked goods give credence to this.

Thank God for people like Jan, who not only love to cook but enjoy sharing their gift with others.

WORK BURDENS

I love my job and my ministry work. I'm involved with Nurses Christian Fellowship and work at an adolescent treatment center, which I also view as ministry. But despite my joy in these areas and the encouragement of a strong support network, there are times when my heart is heavy. The sorrows of others become my sorrows as well, and I have to learn to encourage myself in the Lord while also allowing others to encourage me.

Single adults often have difficult and demanding jobs. We tend to tie our self-worth and competence to our work, and during the times when we feel we're not producing efficiently and effectively, we feel bad about ourselves. Or if we're stuck in a job we hate, we can become depressed. In these cases, a strong personal support network is absolutely necessary. Our friends can ease feelings of loneliness and inadequacy, and even help us to know if it's time to find another job. They can support us through training to change careers and encourage us to pursue our dreams and passions.

Prayer can also make a difference in our workplaces. Pray for that difficult boss or coworker. Watch and see what God will do. Trust God to give you wisdom and strength to obey him. Look also for opportunities to do things that you find rewarding and fulfilling to offset job frustration. Finding volunteer work that I enjoyed helped me cope with a job I was eager to leave at one time.

HOLDING ON TO JESUS

"GOD's reputation is twenty-four-carat gold, with a lifetime guarantee. The decisions of GOD are accurate down to the nth degree."

PSALM 19:9 THE MESSAGE

This God is my God. He is the final word. "I'm single-minded in pursuit of you; don't let me miss the road-signs you've posted. I relish everything you've told me of life, I won't forget a word of it. My soul is starved and hungry, ravenous!—insatiable for your nourishing commands."

PSALM 119:10, 16, 20 THE MESSAGE

My friend Luisa's job had become almost unbearable. She dreaded going to work. She felt like she was just going through the motions in a job unrelated to her passion of having a business of her own.

Sure it paid the bills and she was grateful, but then the monotony and unfulfillment started to wear on her. She sought out other positions at her workplace, but to no avail. Luisa was wise enough not to leave without God's approval, which she sensed she did not have. She waited, worked diligently, looked for other opportunities outside her work setting and prayed. Months went by before her exodus came. She left her job on a good note and was thankful she could move on.

A new friend of mine, Dr. Ann Craig, knows about day to day responsibility as a single Christian woman. She's never been married, and although at times she's wrestled with this reality, she's making the most of her life to God's glory. "Dr. Ann" has been a pediatrician for sixteen years and loves her work. "I have five thousand kids," she says with a big smile.

Dr. Ann has gone on several mission trips, most recently to Cameroon in central Africa where she, along with nine other doctors, two dentists and two nurses, saw more than four thousand patients in ten days. God has made Psalm 16:6 a reality in her life: "The lines have fallen to me in pleasant places; Indeed, my heritage is beautiful to me." In a quiet, reflective voice she says:

> Singleness is not just a stopping-off point. The Lord has a wonderful plan for us as single Christian women. I've been blessed by the things I'm able to do that I never could have done as a wife and mother—mission work, a busy pediatric practice, being a deaconess in my church and member of the praise team.
>
> With time, I see the wonder of how wise the Lord is in not having me marry or become a mom. Although at age twenty-five I experienced real heartache in not bearing my own kids, I see the abundant life he's given me, including wisdom. I love what I know and have learned through life experiences.

During my short visit with Dr. Ann, I can see that her life exemplifies her words. As she continues to pursue the Lord, her words and actions attest to her commitment to him. Praise God for Dr. Ann's impact on the kingdom of God.

HEALTH ISSUES

I was away from home at a conference when I had the second and worst asthma attack I've ever had—in the middle of the night. As my roommate, whom I hardly knew, slept peacefully, I spent most of the night awake trying to breathe. I wondered if I was taking my last breaths.

I was tempted to panic, which usually accompanies difficulty breathing, but I knew that one of the best things I could do for myself was to stay calm. So silently I prayed. I thanked God for his goodness to me throughout my life and expressed my gratitude for his help.

During those endless hours I felt isolated from human relationships but keenly aware of God's presence. I could feel his comfort as he drew me close to himself. My relationship with him grew immensely in that one night.

The next day I checked my messages at my home. My friend Ginni had called thirty minutes before my asthma attack. She had left one message, and when I didn't respond, she kept calling. I could hear the concern in her voice on the answering machine as she told me she was worried about me and wanted to know that I was OK.

Ginni is also my spiritual daughter. God has knit our hearts together and revealed to us the special work he's doing in each other's lives. She often calls to check on me even though she leads a busy life as a wife and mother of six children. It's one of the many ways she shows her care for me.

I called Ginni the next day to share what had happened. My heart was encouraged that the Lord would put me on her heart in such a way. I'm grateful for who Ginni is in my life and for her prayers that helped sustain me throughout that frightening night.

I've heard horror stories about asthma. I know I could live in fear with all kinds of awful possibilities hanging over my head, but I choose not to, by God's grace and strength. I remain aware of my health issues while not dwelling on them. I know what I need to do to take care of myself and I practice those disciplines while otherwise living a normal life. I am reminded often by the Holy Spirit that my life is in God's hands, that he will accomplish what concerns me (Psalm 31:14-15; 138:8).

My friend Ann, who earlier testified to God's provision of a car, also shared a time when her health was in danger and she was alone:

> After several days of thinking that I had pulled a muscle in the calf of my left leg, I finally went to the hospital, where doctors discovered a blood clot, or deep vein thrombosis, behind my left knee. It was potentially life-threatening. I was alone at the hospital and I tried not to panic as I waited for admittance. In fact, I was rather calm—considering that my life was in danger.
>
> The next day, while still in the hospital, I did have a meltdown, a good cry. When I realized that I couldn't handle the details of this situation on my own, I phoned a good friend who stepped in and drove me home from the hospital. She also took care of getting my big truck from the hospital parking lot to my home.
>
> Scripture tells us in Isaiah 30:18, "Therefore the Lord longs to be gracious to you. And therefore He waits on high to have compassion on you." My Heavenly Father vividly showed me the truth of this verse in this crisis in my life.

As we allow God to provide for our needs, we observe his faithfulness. When we practice a lifestyle of prayer, each time a need arises, we will respond with less worry and greater trust. I will be forever indebted to my family and friends for the way they cared for my mama and me when she was sick and dying. Their presence soothed my broken heart and helped maintain my physical body.

A HELPING HAND

God does care about our needs, all of them. Nothing is too small or too big for his caring heart. This truth brings me great comfort, for I know that I can come to him about anything and he welcomes me. He feels the same way about you too.

I also know that sometimes the care—or lack thereof—we receive from others doesn't feel gracious. Sometimes when we've been hurt badly, we think it would be easier to just go it alone, but we don't need to. As one single adult to another, I encourage you to prayerfully consider two or three people with whom you could develop a trusting relationship. People you would feel comfortable sharing your heart with and who would also share theirs. People you can call, if need be, at four in the morning. A healthy support system involves relationships that are mutually beneficial, full of respect and filled with desire to see one another grow in Christlikeness. As the body of Christ we need to embrace and encourage one another to live well before God and people.

QUESTIONS FOR REFLECTION OR DISCUSSION

1. Describe a typical day in your life as a single adult.

2. What challenges do you face with your finances?

3. Share your experiences with car and transportation issues.

4. What joys and challenges do you have in communicating with your family?

5. How does what you eat affect your life?

6. What work burdens are you facing these days?

7. Are you dealing with any health issues? If so, what help do you need?

Intimacy with God

To the love of my life,

Thank you for being who you are. Thank you for your great and undying love for me. I feel unworthy of it but am so grateful to have it. No other love compares to yours—you outlove them all. Thank you for accepting me, weaknesses and all. Thank you for never leaving me alone to wander aimlessly. Thank you for being my very purpose for living. When everyone else walks away, you remain. Thank you.

You are faithful and true to your word. I don't ever have to worry about you lying to me. I can count on you through long and lonely nights to be with me—in fact, to never leave me. You are my constant companion. Most people long for loyal companionship; I have found mine in you. My one true love, how can I ever thank you for loving me the way you do? I am overjoyed that I will be with you for all of eternity. "Whom have I in heaven but You? And besides You I desire nothing on earth. My flesh and my heart may fail, but God is the strength of my heart and my portion forever" (Psalm 73:25-26). "And though I have not seen you, I love you, and though I do not see you now, I rejoice with joy inexpressible and full of glory" (1 Peter 1:8).

I love you.

I've never had a beautiful engagement ring or stunning wedding dress. I've never had a handsome, loving groom standing at my side. I've never had a large home, expensive car or beautiful children. And yet I have experienced the greatest romance anyone could ever hope for. I once thought of buying a wedding dress, choosing attendants and holding a marriage ceremony between my Lord and me. After the ceremony I would have a wonderful reception of celebration, with professional wedding pictures. What a magnificent portrayal that would be of the love I share with my Lord. Maybe one day I'll do it. If so, you're invited.

I have found Jesus Christ to be enough for me. My relationship and commitment to him have been tested over and over, and he has kept me. I want to remain hidden in the intimate places of his love. The longer I walk with God, the closer he draws me to himself. Things and people of this world "grow strangely dim in the light of his glory and grace." It's amazing to see this truth unfold in my life. As long as I'm pursuing God with my whole heart, our love relationship will never grow old. He continues to show me his heart, for "the one who joins himself to the Lord is one spirit with Him" (1 Corinthians 6:17), and "for us there is but one God, the Father, from whom are all things and we exist for Him" (1 Corinthians 8:6).

How incomprehensible it is that the God of the universe desires a personal relationship with me. And not only with me, but with all who humbly come to him and receive the salvation that only he can give. God is gracious and good. The invitation to walk in singleness is now a deep desire for me. Intimacy with God is the highlight of my life. Growing in that intimacy is worth any trial or sorrow.

THE BEST THING THAT EVER HAPPENED TO ME

In eternity, I will see Jesus Christ face to face. I long to be with him. A personal relationship with him is the best thing that ever happened to me, as a favorite song, "The Best Thing" by Avalon, so beautifully conveys.

God uses music to help me understand who he is and what he means to me. He speaks to me through the lyrics and arrangements of many songs, and I believe he placed a love of music within me for this very purpose. Music offers its own unique connection to the Lord. He uses it to comfort me, instruct me and bring me joy.

Several years ago, I started thinking about what my life would look like if I truly lived with an eternal perspective. That process produced in me a longing to be with Jesus face to face and an awareness that the earth is not my home; I'm just passing through. I like the word *sojourner* because the name communicates the way I try to live my life, with an eternal perspective. I know this is my temporary dwelling place. Philippians 3:20 reminds me that my citizenship is in heaven.

With this mindset, each day is now an adventure and one step closer to home. I have lots to look forward to. Heaven seems more like home since my mother is there. But I also have to remind myself that I'm still on earth, and as the saying goes, I don't want to be so heavenly minded that I'm no earthly good. While I'm here, I want my life to count for Jesus, but when it's time for me to go, you can bet I'll be ready.

My life verse is Philippians 1:21: "For to me to live is Christ and to die is gain." This verse spurs me on to live my earthly life for Christ while I plan for my heavenly life. One day I will finally be home, my real home. In the meantime, God has "made known to me the path of life" and keeps filling me with joy in his presence and eternal pleasures from his right hand (Psalm 16:11 NIV). I praise him with my whole heart.

GROWING INTIMACY WITH GOD

Intimacy is a close relationship between two people who trust each other enough to share their innermost thoughts and feelings. Can God trust me enough to share his inner thoughts and feelings with me? Do I trust him enough to share my inner thoughts and feelings with him? Proverbs 9:10 reminds us that "knowledge of the Holy One is understanding." The more I understand God and his ways, the more I get to know him.

I've been on this journey of walking with God a long time now. I became a Christian at the early age of seven. My parents carried me to church from infancy, and I am forever indebted to them for my early foundation in the faith. My pastor and spiritual father, Rev. J. J. Strickland, was the one who led me to Christ. I had heard him preach about Jesus from the time I could understand speech, and when I came to my seven-year-old understanding of who Jesus was and his purpose for coming, I went forward and yielded my life to him. I am thankful for the journey the Lord and I have shared. He is my reason for living.

Christ seems to be my coworker Florence's reason for living also. I asked her about her experience of intimacy with God as a single Christian woman. To her, intimacy with God is simply spending time with him getting to know him—talking, communicating and fellowshiping:

> We were created to have intimacy with God. The Bible says Adam and Enoch walked with God and had fellowship with him. When Adam broke fellowship with God, he lost the intimacy, which is why God asked Adam where he was in the cool of the day. Adam hid—the result of broken fellowship.
>
> We maintain our intimacy with God by faith, by knowing he's omnipresent, by fellowship with other believers and by romancing the Word of God (John 1:1). "Romancing the word" involves reading, meditating and listening for the Word to speak back to you.
>
> The Holy Spirit encourages me to continually develop my intimacy with God. The Spirit is my helper, partner, collaborator and aid in my spiritual walk. Intimacy with God doesn't mean you have to wake up daily and pray for two hours, but you communicate with him throughout the day.

HOLDING ON TO JESUS

My friend Linda Cloer gave me permission to share a prayer she wrote that captures Christ's love for us.

My Dear Child,

I want to tell you how much I love you. (Ephesians 3:17-19)

I want to take care of you and provide for you. (Matthew 6:25-33)

Nothing you can do can change my love for you. (2 Timothy 1:9)

You see, I love you so much, I died for you. (Romans 5:8)

I will always be with you no matter where you go. (Psalm 139:7-12)

I'm even going ahead of you, so that I can prepare a place just for you.
*   (John 14:1-3)*

I promise I will always love you (Jeremiah 31:3) and will never leave you.
*   (Hebrews 13:5)*

One day we will be together for eternity, and I can hardly wait.
*   (John 17:24)*

Until then, watch for me. (Matthew 24:42)

I will be back for you soon. (Revelation 22:20)

> *With all my heart,*
> *Your bridegroom,*
> *Jesus*

ABIDING

Jesus tells us in the gospel of John, "If you keep My commandments, you will abide in My love; just as I have kept My Father's commandments and abide in His love" (John 15:10). If I obey God, I continue, dwell, am present and remain in his love. When I disobey him, I'm tempted to question his love for me. He doesn't change, I do. I want to remain in his love. I make it my "ambition, whether at home or absent, to be pleasing to Him" (2 Corinthians 5:9).

All of us have to figure out what avenues help us develop and maintain an abiding life. We can try several different disciplines to keep ourselves focused on the Lord. Writing poetry can help us express feelings and thoughts creatively, help us get things out there for God to make sense of. Try it, even if it's for your eyes only. We can also sing to the Lord to express our need for him, acknowledge his presence and enhance our feeling of connectedness to him.

Prayer, talking and listening to God, keeps the communication lines open between us and him. Abiding means resting in his love for us. It means trusting in his love. It means experiencing his love on an emotional level. Journaling our prayer life has a way of clearing the head and heart. And even though journaling may be harder for you than it is for others, trying it may prove beneficial.

Sharing Christ with others also helps us abide in him; it reminds us of who he is and what he's done for us. We're drawn closer to him as we testify about him to someone else. Martha, a young lady that I mentor, shared about her intimacy with God and what abiding means to her. Her testimony reflects those times when we don't feel so close to God:

> I first began feeling distant from God when I didn't hear him speak or feel him move in my quiet times. I would try to read his Word but would end up simply reading the words without really understanding what God was trying to say to me. When I prayed, I felt as if I was just talking; sometimes I couldn't even find much to say.
>
> At first when I noticed these changes, I chalked it up to being tired and thought the next day would be better. But when the next day wasn't better and days turned into weeks, I became worried. What was going on? Why was I feeling this way? What had I done? I began to feel confused about everything. The longer the Lord was silent, the more distant I felt. Then I be-

came scared. I began to realize what an awesome gift it is to be close to the Lord, to feel him work in your life.

Thus began the process of searching my heart for the reason of this dryness. I was able to trace the confusion back to a set of events related to a relationship. My boyfriend and I had been struggling with physical issues, and I knew that I had been gratifying my sinful nature instead of being led by the Spirit. I realized that this was the time I had begun to feel distant from the Lord. I had been slowly slipping into a sinful lifestyle because I was filled with lust. I became worried that I would keep ignoring the Holy Spirit and my heart would become hard, and then I wouldn't care what the Lord wanted me to do. That's when the confusion set in. Should I continue in this relationship?

The most frightening thing about this whole experience was that it happened so slowly, it was gradual and sneaky. Before I knew it, I was in such a funk that I didn't know which way was up. Once I was honest with myself and realized that I wasn't being godly, I felt unworthy to even come before the Lord.

A sweet friend opened her heart to me by listening and giving me guidance. She gave me a small devotional to help me get back on track spending time with the Lord after such an empty time. I was doing one of these devotions when the Lord hit me with truth. I realized that I had been trying to do the "right" things without the Lord, constantly trying to live in a way pleasing to him without his help. I wanted to "prove" to him that I could be good without him having to tell me to do the right thing.

Now the Lord is teaching me that knowing him is walking with him obediently, not merely trying to prove myself to him. This dry time has been a blessing because of what the Lord has shown me. I believe he led me through the desert to open my eyes to the fact that he loves me and I need him.

Martha's struggle, her time of dryness and of restoration, show forth God's love. Throughout Scripture God speaks of his love for his people. Let his Word speak deeply into your heart. Take the words and personalize them. Allow the Holy Spirit to minister to you. Romans 8:35-39 ministers to me on a deep, felt level. From *The Message*, it goes like this:

Do you think anyone is going to be able to drive a wedge between us and Christ's love for us? There is no way! Not trouble, not hard times, not hatred, not hunger, not homelessness, not bullying threats, not backstabbing, not even the worst sins listed in Scripture:

"They kill us in cold blood because they hate you.

We're sitting ducks; they pick us off one by one."

None of this fazes us because Jesus loves us. I'm absolutely convinced that nothing—nothing living or dead, angelic or demonic, today or tomorrow, high or low, thinkable or unthinkable—absolutely nothing can get between us and God's love because of the way that Jesus our Master has embraced us.

I need the constant assurance of God's love for me. That's what keeps me strong and vibrant in my love for him.

GROWING CLOSER

How do we nurture important human relationships? The answer to this question may suggest possibilities of ways to nurture our relationship with God. Adoring him is the first step—adoring him for who he is. Instead of asking him for something, we can tell him how much we love and appreciate him for who he is. For example, Psalm 145:1-3 says,

I will extol You, my God, O King,

And I will bless Your name forever and ever.

Every day I will bless You,
And I will praise Your name forever and ever.
Great is the LORD, and highly to be praised,
And His greatness is unsearchable.

Heidi is executive director of Chayil Inc., a ministry to women. She desires to continually grow her intimacy with God but has some unique challenges. Heidi shares:

> Being a survivor of sexual abuse, intimacy with God is an issue. I have a hard time trusting. I want to free-fall into God's arms, but I'm afraid of being hurt. Yet I realize that I must have an intimate relationship with God before I can have true intimacy with a man. I have come to accept this as a part of my journey and I pray daily that I may walk with my hand in God's.

According to Gary Chapman, author of *The Five Love Languages*, we each have a primary avenue by which we give and receive love. The five love languages are words of affirmation, quality time, gifts, acts of service and physical touch. When we receive ample amounts of love in our primary language, our "love tank" remains full, Chapman says.

Dr. Ross Campbell, who specializes in the treatment of children and adolescents, also uses the metaphor of a love tank in his book *The Five Love Languages of Children* (which he coauthored with Gary Chapman). He says, "Inside every child is an 'emotional tank' waiting to be filled with love. When a child really feels loved, he will develop normally, but when the love tank is empty, the child will misbehave. Much of the misbehavior of children is motivated by the cravings of an empty 'love tank.'"

One of Chapman's latest works is *The Love Languages of God*. He suggests three questions we can ask to help discover our love language:

1. How do I most often express love to other people?

2. What do I complain about most often?

3. What do I request most often?

Once we discover our primary love language in human relationships, Chapman says, we can assume that this is also our primary love language in our relationship with God.

As I see it, not only do we receive love best from God in our love language, we also express love best to him in that same language, which can help our intimacy with him deepen. When I first got Chapman's book, I read it excitedly, eager to find out God's love language towards me. I wasn't surprised to learn that it was words of affirmation. This realization helped me see why I have such a passion for God's Word. I love to read his words to me and to all of us. I love to journal, writing back to him. I enjoy sending and receiving notes from others. When I write, I feel close to God.

Our spiritual health as Christians depends upon intimacy with God. We must guard against abandoning our first love (Revelation 2:4). When it's all said and done, God's love remains. I pray that we will know this love more and more deeply, his love shed abroad in our hearts through the Holy Spirit (Romans 5:5).

As we cultivate our love relationship with God, we will be examples to the world around us that we serve a personal God. Others will see for themselves that our beliefs are genuine and that they can share that intimacy too. Intimacy with God creates a belief system that matches up with our lifestyle. This is my desire, that my lips won't speak what my life does not exclaim. This is my prayer:

Lord, I want to delight myself in you, to find my joy in you at all times. I want to have a reputation for gentleness and never forget the nearness of you. I don't want to worry about anything; instead I want to pray about everything in a thankful way. I want to experience your peace, which is far more wonderful than the human mind can understand. I know that your peace will keep my heart and my thoughts quiet and at rest as I trust Jesus. Hallelujah! Amen! I want to fix my mind on what is true, good, right, pure and beautiful. I want to think about all that I can praise you for.

QUESTIONS FOR REFLECTION OR DISCUSSION

1. Describe the love of your life.

2. How would you respond to the statement, "Jesus Christ is enough for me"?

3. How would you define intimacy? What intimacy busters do you experience on a regular basis?

4. In what ways does music move you to greater intimacy with God? What song would you choose to describe your walk with God?

5. Reflect on what it means for you to abide in Christ.

6. Describe a dry time in your spiritual life and how you overcame it.

7. What does it mean for you to have a love relationship with God? In what ways does it need to grow?

8. Although you may have never read *The Five Love Languages*, after seeing what they are, what would you say is your primary love language and why?

9. How does your love language work in your relationship with God?

We're Got a Reason to Celebrate

You're Invited
To a party for Jesus!

Where:
Everywhere you go

When:
All the time

Why?
Because he is worthy

W hat would it look like to throw a party for Jesus? Would there be balloons and a cake? Gifts, music and dancing? Actually, as we celebrate Christ, setting him apart as Lord in our hearts, we are throwing a party for him. By our lives, we can show how important he is to us and that we want to bring him joy.

Your response may be, "Celebrate? What do I have to celebrate? Not too many people seem interested in celebrating my singleness with me." I'm not asking you to celebrate your singleness; I'm asking you to celebrate Christ in you, our hope of glory. He is our reason to celebrate. Apart from him, no Christian has a reason to celebrate. He is our purpose in life. Apart from him, we have no reason for living. We worship, celebrate and adore him because he is worthy of our highest praise.

ETERNAL PRAISE

Scripture is replete with admonitions to praise God and reasons for why we should do so. Deuteronomy 33:27 says,

The eternal God is a dwelling place,
And underneath are the everlasting arms;
And He drove out the enemy from before you,
And said, "Destroy!"

Our eternal God is our dwelling place and his everlasting arms shelter us. How many times has he moved our enemy from before us? He deserves eternal praise because of his faithfulness to care for us. He never stops planning his care for his own.

When Jesus spoke to the crowds, many of his disciples said his words were too hard. And many walked away. Jesus then turned to his twelve closest followers: you're not going too, are you? "Simon Peter answered Him, 'Lord, to whom shall we go? You have words of eternal life'" (John 6:68). Jesus died so that everyone on earth could hear his words of eternal life, which give us eternity in heaven and a taste of heaven on earth right now. In John 17:3, Jesus says, "This is eternal life, that they may know You, the only true God, and Jesus Christ whom You have sent."

The apostle Paul encourages an eternal perspective in 2 Corinthians 4:18, which tells us to "look not at the things which are seen, but at the things which are not seen; for the things which are seen are temporal, but the things which are not seen are eternal." Single adults are constantly, blatantly reminded of their single status—a temporal thing—and sometimes the church is the worst offender. As the body of Christ, we need to encourage an eternal perspective, not an earthly focus. May we support each other in setting our affections on things above, as written in Colossians 3:1. As we maintain an eternal perspective, we will cultivate an attitude of eternal praise for all of God's good gifts to us.

HOLDING ON
TO JESUS

According to 2 Corinthians 4:17,
"Momentary, light affliction
is producing for us an eternal
weight of glory far beyond all
comparison." An eternal weight
of glory sounds like a lot to me,
far beyond our imagination.
What is your momentary, light
affliction today? Does it seem long
term instead of momentary?
Does it seem heavy instead of
light? Our eternal God extends to
us eternal words. When we receive
them, we're able to see that our
affliction on earth is producing for
us an eternal weight of glory. And
our soul can shout "Hallelujah!"

He has done it all for us, that we may show forth the praise of his glory: "Now to the King eternal, immortal, invisible, the only God, be honor and glory forever and ever. Amen" (1 Timothy 1:17). Amazingly, we have a mediator who is also a best friend: "For by the power of the eternal Spirit, Christ offered himself to God as a perfect sacrifice for our sins. That is why he is the one who mediates the new covenant between God and people, so that all who are invited can receive the eternal inheritance God has promised them" (Hebrews 9:14-15 NLT). Another cause for eternal praise!

In Psalm 102:18 we read, "This will be written for the generation to come, / That a people yet to be created may praise the LORD." We are the generations to come. Our praise for God was foretold. We're expected to praise him. The psalmist wrote these words in particular that we might praise God, but God's Word overall reminds us of our need to continually praise our God. In celebrating Jesus Christ, we take our eyes off of ourselves, others and everything else, and we place them on him. With our eyes on him we can't help but celebrate, because we see him for who he is.

PURSUING GOD

How else can we keep celebrating Jesus? By remaining attentive to his will for our lives. By staying in constant contact with him through prayer. By consecrating and keeping ourselves ready for him, listening for his voice. By dedicating our life to him, acknowledging unashamedly that we belong to him. By proclaiming him whenever we have the opportunity.

To feast upon the Lord is to draw our nourishment from him. We look to him for all we need in life—spiritually, emotionally, mentally and physically. We learn to rejoice in him regardless of our circumstances. When we do this, we learn that joy is not circumstantial but relational—it comes through relating with Christ. In celebrating Jesus, we learn to let loose and let go. We totally abandon and surrender ourselves to his will, abiding in the life he has given us through his death. Psalm 84:5-7 sums it up:

> Happy are those who are strong in the LORD,
>   who set their minds on a pilgrimage to Jerusalem.
> When they walk through the Valley of Weeping,
>   it will become a place of refreshing springs,
>   where pools of blessing collect after the rains!
> They will continue to grow stronger,
>   and each of them will appear before God in Jerusalem. (NLT)

DISCIPLESHIP

Love is the key to bringing others to Christ and helping them grow in him. The world will know we are Christians by our love for one another. They will also know we are Christians by the love we show them. We show people love by listening to them, helping with practical needs, and offering words of encouragement and prayer, to name a few.

Love and acceptance go hand in hand. As I show love to someone else, I am communicating acceptance. I know that I am accepted in Christ, so as I accept and love another person, I honor him. Granted, some people are just hard to love, and it can be difficult to know the difference between accepting someone and condoning their behavior. But as we keep our eyes on Christ, he shows us the way.

We also honor Christ by using the gifts and talents he's given us. Our abilities can be used in many ways—serving in our local church, volunteering in our communities and being faithful in our work. We can use our talents creatively with every person we meet, specifically when we share our faith. If we are born again, something should be different in our lives; those who are in Christ are new creations (2 Corinthians 5:17).

I am thankful for my new life in Christ. After years of walking with Jesus, I trust I am looking more like him. Perfect? No. Growing? Yes. As I grow, I act more like a beloved child of God. I act like I have a new Father and a new citizenship. Things start to look different in my world. I start to sound different. I belong to a new family, the family of God. Christ is honored when his people act like family, a healthy family with him as head. I rejoice in my God and his salvation (Psalm 9:14; 21:1).

Christ is honored in me when I know him not just in salvation but in lordship. Studying the attributes of God is one of the most, if not *the*, most rewarding use of my time. Looking at who he really is enlarges my heart and my faith in him, making me more aware of his presence. Colossians 3:1-4 describes his lordship in our lives:

> Since you have been raised to new life with Christ, set your sights on the realities of heaven, where Christ sits at God's right hand in the place of honor and power. Let heaven fill your thoughts. Do not think only about things down here on earth. For you died when Christ died, and your real life is hidden with

Christ in God. And when Christ, who is your real life, is revealed to the whole world, you will share in all his glory. (NLT)

THE LIVING WORD

God's Word is another reason to celebrate. It speaks truth into our
lives. Because of his Word, we learn who we are, who he is and how
to live a life that's pleasing to him. In Psalm 119:162, the psalmist
declares, "I rejoice in your word like one who finds a great treasure"
(NLT). I too rejoice in God's Word and have found it to be a great
treasure.

> Everyone will share the story of your wonderful goodness;
> they will sing with joy of your righteousness.
> The LORD is kind and merciful, slow to get angry, full of
>   unfailing love.
> The LORD is good to everyone. He showers compassion on
>   all his creation.
> All of your works will thank you, LORD,
> and your faithful followers will bless you. (Psalm 145:7-10 NLT)

Truly, "whoever believes in him will not be disappointed" (Romans
10:11).

A LIFESTYLE OF WORSHIP

Living a lifestyle of worship demonstrates God's worthiness to receive
all honor and praise. Worship is more than going to church for a service. Our speech, actions and attitude display our worship. If someone spent time with you for ten minutes, would that person be able
to tell that you were a true worshiper of Jesus Christ—not a make-
shift worshiper, someone with a fake smile and a false "hallelujah and
praise the Lord"? Hopefully they see a genuine person with a heart
full of love for the Savior they've never seen, but whom they continually experience through the Holy Spirit.

A true worshiper has the Holy Spirit flowing on the inside and over-flowing on the outside with love for Jesus and others. A true worshiper is humble with no need to prove anything. A true worshiper's sole purpose is to bring God pleasure, to make sure he is satisfied. Proverbs 9:10 states, "The fear of the LORD is the beginning of wisdom." The fear of the Lord is reverence for him. As we learn to revere him above all else, our wisdom will grow. We will learn how to please him.

Psalm 29:1-2, 33:3 and 66:1-3 demonstrate ways we can please him. We can give him honor in word and deed. We can praise his glory and strength, realizing there is no one like him—no other glory, no other strength. Philippians 2:9-10 tells us that Christ's name is above every other name, and that one day at his name every knee will bow and every tongue will confess that he is Lord, to the glory of his Father.

Knowing this, we can sing to the Lord a new song. What new songs has he given you lately, songs that encourage you and draw you to worship? Has he put his own special song in your heart? If so, maybe you should write it out and sing it over and over. Shout joy-fully to God, even when it doesn't feel good. Usually praise helps lift us from a downward spiral of discouragement. Sing the glory of his name. Sing what his name represents. Tell him and the world around you how glorious he is. Focusing on his attributes helps us know him for who he is, and he is glorious. Tell God how awesome his works are. Brag about him. He brags about you!

LEGACIES OF CELEBRATION

The thought of leaving a legacy of praise thrills my heart. As you think about what your legacy will be, reflect on the following ques-tions:

- What will people remember the most about you when you're gone?

- What do you want them to remember?
- What does your life communicate about your single status?
- What words of wisdom and encouragement do you have for those who come after you who may be single a long time or forever? Will they look to you for advice and for comfort?

After hearing me share about my singleness in a positive light, a young woman approached me with excitement. She exclaimed, "I'm so glad to hear you say these things. I once heard a single woman speak and she talked about how hard the single life was. She was so negative she frightened me. Thank you for your encouragement." This young woman encouraged me too—it's rare for me to get that kind of enthusiastic response. In my forty-nine years of living single, I'd met maybe two other unmarried adults who were as excited about being single as I was. One of these women enthusiastically asked about the possibility of starting a support group for people who believe God wants them to remain single. I'd never thought of such a thing. I couldn't believe my ears. The words of these young women were like a refreshing rain.

Evelyn is a sixty-year-old career missionary, widowed with children. She has been single for seventeen years. Listen to her words.

> No, I do not want to be married. Caring for a husband would not afford me the freedom that I have to serve the Lord and his people. I would not be able to pick up and go whenever or wherever I am needed. Nor could I minister to women in my home at my discretion.

Evelyn is leaving an encouraging legacy for other women who choose to remain single. But you don't have to be a missionary to offer hope to others through your life. There are many rewarding ways to leave a legacy. Consider the following ideas:

- Keep a diary of feelings, thoughts and events you wouldn't mind someone finding and reading.

- Keep a prayer journal with requests and answers.

- Keep letters, articles and even e-mails.

- Keep a scrapbook with family photos, recipes and stories, and write down memories of each period of your life. Include details about best friends, events, homes and so on.

- Interview elderly parents and other relatives and record their memories either in written form or on videotape.

I had the privilege of writing my mom's life story before she died. I had been collecting information from her for over twelve years, and once I completed the project, I rushed it to a local printing company and had two copies made so my mother could see her story before she died. Before I sold her home and moved out, I had someone videotape the house so I could hold on to some memories in that way.

Mossi, my colleague and sister in Christ, died recently. A testimony given at her memorial service blessed me so greatly that I asked Julie, Mossi's colleague who gave it, for permission to reproduce it. Here's what Julie said:

> I appreciated how Mossi lived out her singleness. I'm single, and I know that some places you go, people make you feel like half a couple! Mossi never seemed like half a couple. There was a fullness of life and joy in her, in her home and in her relationships, that I appreciated. She was a mentor in this way, and as long as God gives me the gift of enjoying life as a single woman, I hope I can live it out as fully as my sister did.

Like Mossi did so effectively, we have to guard against negative attitudes, people and behaviors that hinder our leaving a legacy for God's glory. And the best way to guard against such negativity is to develop an attitude of gratitude. As we focus on God's goodness to us, appreciating him and his blessings, our attitudes lift.

Life really is short. We need to make every moment count,

whether in times of seriousness or fun. We have frequent opportunities to share the things we've learned with other people so that we can make a difference in their lives. God satisfies us with good things through the years so that our youthfulness remains. We don't need anti-aging cream in the spiritual realm, because the Holy Spirit of God preserves us. He enables and empowers us to live life according to God's perfect plan for us and to accomplish his purposes. Our God is good. He is mindful of us.

Loretta has been a single career missionary for ten years. She's committed to God's call on her life. She celebrates Jesus as a single Christian woman in her response to his call with joy and gratitude. Her mission statement communicates her vision: "Be a disciple of Christ and go make disciples for Christ." She is presently serving her second year with Carver International Missions as resource development officer. To become better equipped for the work, she is pursuing a master's degree in missiology. She has a burden for the Somali people and especially Muslim women. Loretta says:

> For the most part, I enjoy my life as a single missionary. There have been some struggles, challenges and lows, but I've learned to press through them and allow God's hand to mold and shape me into his servant. There are seasons, days and moments when I love being in the position I am and truly enjoy the experience of being single, saved and satisfied. I tell the Lord, "Oh, I don't want to give this up." My life is adventurous as a missionary servant of Christ Jesus and I like that. It's great when I experience his power, grace and love in awesome ways. I'm growing in discipleship as I serve in missions.

Although her contentment is obvious, Loretta does desire marriage, believing it would enhance her ministry. She's trusting God for a mate with whom she can be equally yoked.

I enjoy the work I do for the Lord. Part of my prayer request when praying for a mate is that he too would be involved and we would enjoy a missions ministry together.

IT IS WELL WITH MY SOUL

Harriette works at one my favorite Christian bookstores. She always greets me with a smile and word of encouragement. Harriette has two children and has been single again for sixteen years. I asked her to tell me reasons she celebrates the hope that is within her, and this is what she had to say:

> I celebrate because of the assurance in knowing Christ dwells within me. I believe what the Scriptures teach about Christ and I have experienced his power in my life; I have seen his promises at work. I trust him because he's faithful. In times of fear, alone and without a partner, when I don't know what will happen, I have experienced Christ's sufficiency and the peace only he can give.
>
> I look forward to seeing what God will do every day, because I know he's at work every day. One day a lady came into the bookstore looking for a particular song. We just happened to have the song playing. That morning, the person in charge of the music had put that song in even though it's one we don't usually play. I see God laughing sometimes because he has a treat and surprise waiting for us and he can't wait for us to see it. God loves us and wants what's best for us. He wants us to acknowledge daily his activity in our lives. I get excited at the store seeing God at work as I interact with people, some who are hurting. I'm also encouraged at seeing the customers interact and care for each other. I say, "Thank you, God, for letting me see you in the crises and in the little things day by day."
>
> In teaching a Sunday school class of ninety-year-olds and

plus, I see their joy in living. They remind me that even as I age, I can look forward to each new day. I see where they've been and they are still full of life, hope and trust. They, along with my ninety-three-year-old mother, inspire me. And although my mother has had her share of heartaches, she's not depressed or down on life. So even as I age and my body changes, I don't have to dread getting older because I trust in the Lord. I have a peace walking with the Lord that is very real.

Like these inspiring women, I continually celebrate the hope that is within me. Praise God, it is well with my soul because I know the one who keeps my heart. I'm thankful that he does work all things together for my good because I love him and am called according to his purpose (Romans 8:28). Likewise, Jeremiah 9:23-24 says, "Let not a wise man boast of his wisdom, and let not the mighty man boast of his might, let not a rich man boast of his riches; but let him who boasts boast of this, that he understands and knows Me, that I am the LORD who exercises lovingkindness, justice and righteousness on earth; for I delight in these things."

I want these verses to penetrate my heart, my very soul. They hold the key to celebrating Christ and his life in me. May the words of this hymn, penned by Horatio Spafford after losing his business and children, sink deep into the soil of your heart. God bless you as you seek to honor him as a single adult, for such a time as this (Esther 4:14).

When peace like a river,
attendeth my way,
when sorrows like sea billows roll—
whatever my lot,
thou hast taught me to say,
it is well, it is well
with my soul.

It is well with my soul
It is well, it is well with my soul.

Tho Satan should buffet,
tho trials should come,
let this blest assurance control,
that Christ hath regarded my helpless estate
and shed His own blood for my soul.
It is well with my soul
It is well, it is well with my soul.

And, Lord, haste the day
when my faith shall be sight,
the clouds be rolled back
as a scroll:
The trump shall resound and
the Lord shall descend,
"Even so"—it is well with my soul.
It is well with my soul,
It is well, it is well with my soul.

QUESTIONS FOR REFLECTION OR DISCUSSION

1. How do you feel when you think about celebrating Jesus Christ?

2. What makes God's Word a reason to celebrate?

3. Describe your eternal perspective at this season of your life.

4. How does your life reflect a lifestyle of worship?

5. If you were at the end of your life, what kind of legacy of celebration would you leave?

6. Is it well with your soul? Why or why not?

A P P E N D I X

Ideas for Churches that Want to Reach Singles

The American Association for Single People reports these findings: "Nearly one half of the adult population in America is unmarried, one out of ten of us is divorced, and one out of four households is occupied by a single person living alone. These findings reflect a thirty-year trend in America to marry later in life, divorce, or never get married at all. There are now more than 80 million adults 18 and older who are single, divorced, or widowed. If we instead start counting at age 15, the number approaches 100 million. Within another eight years, singles will outnumber marrieds."

How can the church help these single adults, who only promise to become greater in number? There are a number of ways to reach this population of the local church for the strength and edification of the body.

IDEAS TO IMPLEMENT

An effective single adult ministry offers support to its people. It also equips single adults in developing Christlikeness to the honor and glory of God. The single adult ministry needs to be an integral part of body life, not leftover ministry.

Encourage interaction between generations. Singles ministry needs to foster activities that lead to intergenerational relationships and create an intergenerational community. Joe and Susan Clamon were single adult directors at their church for many years. Susan says the healthiest single adults are those with relationships across the board, who don't just hang out with single people all the time. They have relationships with married people, divorced people, children, youth and senior adults. Though married now for thirty-five years, the Clamons still feel a call to invest in the lives of single adults because "they have invested so much in us," she says.

Place singles in leadership. Churches can call more single adults into leadership positions, both on a volunteer basis and as part of church staff. Seeing single adults in leadership encourages other single adults who attend the church. Tim Cleary, single adult ministry specialist for LifeWay Christian Resources, says, "The church of the future must be led by both married and single adult leaders, operating in a church culture which includes dual married and single adult models."

Model healthy relationships. People attend church in part to develop encouraging relationships, yet we all know that difficult relationships are a part of everyone's life at some point. Each of us carries around our custom-tailored set of baggage until we let God take the burden. With the help of the local body and its leadership, single adults have the opportunity to see and experience healthy relationships in the name of Christ. Single adult leaders have the privilege of modeling healthy relationships, and they can teach and counsel those God sends to their ministry.

Offer practical assistance. Offering classes appropriate for single adults, such as time and money management, enhances the ministry. The pastoral care ministry has the opportunity to help with practical needs like financial assistance and housing. Once, when my funds were running low, I mustered up enough courage and laid down enough pride to ask my church to help pay my rent. It was a humbling experience; one I hope never to repeat. Unfortunately, I didn't feel much warmth from the counselor who assisted me, but help was granted, and I was grateful for the assistance.

Support single parents. I've heard of some churches that provide specific ministry to single parents, and I applaud them. And although single parents often do not want to be singled out, their role has many challenges. My heart grieves as I observe many single mothers. I wonder what kind of support system they have. A friend of mine who is a single parent with two children was once married to an abusive husband. The Christian community's response was not kind. Single parenting is hard enough without the insensitivity of "well-meaning" Christians. We need to offer support and encouragement to our single parents.

Provide opportunities for fun. Social activities are also important, but I sometimes feel that single adult ministries err too much on the side of entertainment and don't focus enough on time in the Word and discipleship. However, healthy fun is essential.

Confront issues of sexuality. I've never known a singles ministry that dealt head-on with sexuality issues. Maybe this is why so many single Christian adults struggle in this area. I've been grieved by the way the church has dealt with sexuality—or not dealt with it, actually. It's as though leaders are scared to death to deal with such an important subject. I wonder if one of the reasons is that they're not comfortable with their own sexuality. As church leaders, we need to take a long, hard look at how our local body provides ministry in this area.

Plan community meals. Many single adults struggle with having meals alone on a regular basis. I believe this is especially true for women who long to be married and have a family. Meals together on a consistent basis could alleviate the sense of loneliness so many feel in eating alone. I was once part of a single adult ministry that shared Sunday lunch together at a restaurant. That was a fun time of food and fellowship. Churches can also encourage families and single adults to have meals together. This could be a huge ministry to single adults.

Invite single speakers. I was asked to speak at a single women's luncheon hosted by a singles ministry. I had never heard of such a gathering, but the single women seemed encouraged by it. The fee was minimal and single men of the church served the meal. Through such outreach, single adults are touched on a larger scale as we learn from speakers, teachers and one another. The question-and-answer time gave us the opportunity to hear what was on other women's minds and hearts.

Invest in outreach. A single adult ministry provides an incredible opportunity to build up single Christians and equip them to reach others who don't know Christ. Single adults have great potential to advance the kingdom of God. Helping them see their value in this area will bring eternal results to our local body of believers.

SINGLE VOICES

Cathy Meadows attends Perimeter Church in Atlanta. Perimeter's ministry to single adults involves small groups, discipleship, service and mission opportunities, solid biblical teaching, and fun. Cathy says, "We have a desire to bring the younger culture of our church into an authentic encounter with God, each other and themselves, so that God might be magnified and their community and world transformed."

The leaders try to admonish single adults with the reality that whatever fears or unbeliefs they may have about God as singles will follow them into marriage and parenthood. The root problems will be the same even if the circumstances will change. For example, Cathy says, "If I have fear now as a single adult that God won't give me a husband, that fear could transform into a fear that my husband will die or that he will not give me kids."

Caren is a member of a large metropolitan church with a singles group. The mission of this ministry is to offer encouragement to singles and help them know where they're going. They desire to work toward God and his plan, heading in his direction. The group emphasizes prayer in its weekly small group meetings, and an e-mail goes out regularly with information about singles activities. The singles pastor and his wife are approachable and concerned about people in the ministry. Caren says the wife draws people to her, which I believe is an asset to lots of hurting single women.

But there's room for improvement. Caren feels the praise and worship needs pepping up, and the ministry needs to be more focused on goals that enhance unity. Commitment and follow-through also need to be more consistent. She would like to see certain topics addressed, such as how men and women should treat each other, learning how to court again and preparing oneself for marriage. When I asked Caren for a word to encourage single adults, she quoted Matthew 6:33: "But seek first His kingdom and His righteousness, and all these things will be added to you."

GETTING PLUGGED IN

Once church leaders have done the job of nurturing and equipping single adults, they should channel them into ministry areas suitable to their gifts and talents. Single adults have the potential to work in most areas of the church, including children's ministry, music, prayer ministry, counseling, widows ministry, deaf ministry, hospitality, pastoral care, women's ministry, men's ministry, youth ministry, senior adult ministry, outreach, missions, homebound ministry and media ministry. There's a place for everyone. I'm sure there are many more that I haven't thought of.

Single adults want to know they are a part of church life overall. They realize body life is much bigger than singleness, but sometimes they need to be encouraged to integrate into the church. Single adults have much to offer as they go forward in life with Christ's life indwelling. My prayer for the church is that our eyes would stay fixed upon Jesus and all he has in mind for us. I pray we would not shrink back from his call, but would follow him wholeheartedly, trusting his plans for our lives. Thank God for his church, which is called out to nurture and grow its own and then reach out to those nearby, farther away and to the ends of the earth. Praise God for his plans for his people as we walk together in the body of Christ, single and whole.

RESOURCES

Arterburn, Stephen. *Addicted to Love*. Ann Arbor, Mich.: Servant, 2003.

Arterburn, Stephen, and Margaret Rinck. *Avoiding Mr. Wrong*. Nashville: Thomas Nelson, 2000.

———. *Finding Mr. Right*. Nashville: Thomas Nelson, 2001.

Blackaby, Henry. *Experiencing God*. Nashville: Broadman & Holman, 1994.

Carter, Les. *People Pleasers*. Nashville: Broadman & Holman, 2000.

Chapman, Gary. *The Five Love Languages*. Chicago: Moody Press, 1996.

———. *The Five Love Languages of God*. Chicago: Northfield, 2002.

Cloud, Henry, and John Townsend. *Boundaries*. Grand Rapids: Zondervan, 1992.

———. *Safe People*. Grand Rapids: Zondervan, 1995.

Couchman, Judy. *Designing a Woman's Life*. Sisters, Ore.: Multnomah, 1996.

Crabb, Larry. *Connecting*. Nashville: Word, 1997.

DeMoss, Bob. *Sex and the Single Person*. Grand Rapids: Zondervan, 1995.

Dillow, Linda, and Lorraine Pintus. *Gift-Wrapped by God*. Colorado Springs: WaterBrook, 2002.

Frazier, Sundee Tucker. *Finding Wholeness as a Multiracial Person*. Downers Grove, Ill.: InterVarsity Press, 2002.

Goring, Ruth. *Singleness*. Downers Grove, Ill.: InterVarsity Press, 2002.

Harris, Joshua. *I Kissed Dating Goodbye*. Sisters, Ore.: Multnomah Publishers, 1997.

Hsu, Albert Y. *Singles at the Crossroads*. Downers Grove, Ill.: InterVarsity Press, 1997.

Hurnard, Hannah. *Hinds Feet on High Places: A Devotional for Women*. Shippensburg, Penn.: Destiny Image, 1993.

McGee, Robert. *The Search for Significance*. Houston: Rapha Publishing, 1990.

Moore, Beth. *Breaking Free*. Nashville: LifeWay, 1999.

Page, Carole Gift. *Becoming A Woman of Passion*. Grand Rapids: Fleming H. Revell, 2001.

Powell, John. *Why Am I Afraid to Tell You Who I Am?* Allen, Tex.: Thomas More, 1969.

Richardson, Rick. *Sex: What's God Got to Do with It?* Downers Grove, Ill.: InterVarsity Press, 2002.

Seamands, David, *Healing for Damaged Emotions*. Colorado Springs: Chariot Victor, 1991.

Smith, M. Blaine. *Should I Get Married?* Downers Grove, Ill.: InterVarsity Press, 2000.

Springle, Pat. *A Christian Perspective on Codependence*. Houston and Dallas: Rapha Publishing/Word, 1995.

Tieger, Paul D., and Barbara Barron-Tieger. *Do What You Are*. Boston: Little, Brown, 1995.

ONLINE RESOURCES

BakeWorks, Etc. <bakeworksetc@yahoo.com >

Chayil Inc. <www.chayilinc.org>